Foundations of
Modern Jurisprudence

Foundations of
Modern Jurisprudence

by

WILLIAM SEAL CARPENTER
Late of Princeton University

NEW   YORK

Appleton-Century-Crofts, Inc.

347.09
C 22 f
65184
March 1969

Preface

UNDERGRADUATE INSTRUCTION in jurisprudence throughout American colleges and universities has long been unsatisfactory. For the most part courses have been in elementary law or in the philosophy of law. Neither have been of great value to the prospective candidate for the bar. The elements of English common law are best reserved for the law school, where the student must go far beyond the confines of a general survey. American law schools are today providing the most precise and scientific training to be found anywhere at the graduate level. There are no short cuts to the mastery of legal knowledge.

The philosophy of law is interesting, although much is lost when it is detached from general philosophy. However, the student of law who proceeds through the course of study in a modern law school will develop his own philosophy of law. His legal education may be handicapped if he approaches his subject with the philosophic notions of other men too firmly fixed in his mind. The study of the philosophy of law is for the prospective lawyer best left to the last year in the law school.

The service which the study of jurisprudence can best render the undergraduate is to acquaint him with the nature and development of early legal institutions. The rich heritage of the past in legal and political thinking can be of tremendous value in obtaining an understanding of present day law and procedures. Legal thinking comprises remarkably few ideas, which recur in infinite combinations. History provides a method whereby the treasury of past thinking can be observed in correct perspective. Whether the student in college contemplates entering the legal profession or not, his education will be greatly advanced if he knows how men came into possession of their legal institutions.

Jurisprudence cannot be taught from a single textbook. This was attempted in the last century when the analytical school of jurisprudence established a priority for the teachings of John Austin. In our own day no priority can be maintained for any school of jurisprudence much less for a single writer on the subject. The whole range of the social sciences contributes to a legal education, and an historical introduction to the beginnings of legal institutions becomes an appropriate first step in the course of study.

The use of the readings book in the teaching of jurisprudence is now common. Carpenter and Stafford, *Readings in Early Legal Institutions* (New York, Appleton-Century-Crofts, 1932), was prepared to make readily accessible materials designed to promote the study of the historical development of legal institutions. At the same time, any set of readings or excerpts is made more intelligible by adequate commentary. The present volume is offered as a further help in the advancement of this important subject in the education of American undergraduates.

W. S. C.

Princeton University

Contents

Part One

THEORIES AND SYSTEMS
OF LAW

I

The Nature of Jurisprudence

"JURISPRUDENCE IS THE KNOWLEDGE of things divine and human, the knowledge of what is just and what is unjust."[1] This definition of Ulpian was copied by the framers of the Digest of Justinian without, however, accompanying it with the full explanation of the meaning of the terms. This is unfortunate. At first glance, it would appear that jurisprudence is intended to embrace the whole field of human knowledge. But elsewhere it appears that Ulpian, and the other Roman lawyers, expected the subject of jurisprudence to deal with law. In other words, the law was to include those things, whether derived from divine or human sources, which determine the relations of men in society. Behind all human laws was an overruling law of nature. In the words of Cicero, to live according to nature is the highest good.

[1] Definitions of jurisprudence will be found in all textbooks on the subject. Each author is likely to define the term according to his own approach. There is no universal and eternally valid definition; the meaning of the term has varied during the epochs in which it has been used. An excellent dictionary of Roman law terms has appeared recently, A. Berger, *Encyclopedic Dictionary of Roman Law* (Philadelphia, 1953).

The jurist is not, therefore, restricted to a set of rules for the regulation of a particular society. He is required to look beyond the rules of law to discover the purpose which the rules were intended to serve. The purpose of law is the achievement of justice. In all his work, the jurist must recognize in the law the art of the good and the just, and must strive so to formulate his rules that justice will be distinguished from injustice and that men will be inclined toward the good and away from the bad. The science of jurisprudence at any time includes not merely the study of the existing rules of law but also the development of the legal system in accordance with the ultimate law of reason and justice. Human law is not the capricious will of the lawgiver but tends at any rate to apply to the conditions of actual life those principles which are of perpetual obligation.

The relation between law and morals is of transcendant importance in the study of jurisprudence. The content of the law is one of morality. Since law must distinguish between justice and injustice, between good and evil, men for centuries sought to establish a standard by which the validity of human laws could be determined. This was the function of natural law. In all its ramifications the theory of natural law had only one fundamental purpose, to provide an ultimate measure of right and wrong. To the men of the Middle Ages the natural was identified with the divine law, but with Grotius the rules of natural law were valid in themselves, independently of the fact that God willed them. Man is given reason by God, and it is sufficient that the rules which he creates have a purely rational construction. Thus politics and law became separated from theology and acquired independent foundations.

The Roman jurists, from whose writings the Corpus Juris was compiled, did not minutely define the term *law*. To be sure, they set up broad generalizations and classified the kinds of law known at Rome. In the dictionary compiled by Isidore of Seville, the definitions were multiplied and refined. These were subsequently of great value, especially to the churchmen, and served to carry into medieval theories of law and politics more precise statements of fundamental principles than had previously existed.[2]

From the outset, jurisprudence has had a practical as well as an ideal function. To the jurists of republican Rome the arrangement of the rules of praetorian law was an essentially practical task which afforded little time or opportunity for philosophical refinements. The later jurists, who were identified with the rival law schools of the early empire, were not satisfied with exercises in legal classification. Nothing stimulates thought more than controversy. The lawyers of the first three centuries of the Christian era therefore took exuberant delight in formulating their legal rules against a background of philosophical principles. They were careful to wrap their *responsa prudentium*, or opinions binding on the judges, in generalizations which gave breadth and the appearance of learning to their conclusions. Certainly one finds neither great originality nor philosophic depth in these juristic writings. But the work of Papinian, Ulpian, and Paulus undertook to combine the practical with the ideal purposes of the jurist. A body of legal literature was created which served for centuries to guide the development of the law at the same time that it supplied the foundations for the scientific study of jurisprudence.

Although law schools continued to exist in western Europe throughout the Middle Ages, especially in Italy and Provence, it was not until the eleventh and twelfth centuries that a genuine awakening of theory and learning in the field of law occurred. But it was a severely practical task to which the glossators of Bologna and other Italian universities addressed themselves. They were interested in recovering the Roman law from the corrupting influences which had arisen following the death of Justinian. Their dialectical acumen was exercised on the contents of the Corpus Juris. A gloss was made to summarize each text in short sentences. Intricate subjects were reduced to systematic subdivisions. This exercise has been described by Vinogradoff as follows: "Starting

[2] See Isidori Hispalensis Episcopi, *Etymologiorum sive Originum*, 2 vol. (Oxford, 1911), I, Bk. v.

with a general term or wide conception, it indicated the different species subordinated to it, splitting each up into its subdivisions, and following these ramifications of sense and terminology into the most minute details."³ A simple but effective method of study was thus contrived.

The construction of a method of study was less important than the dialectical analyses of texts. The glossators desired to free the law from uncertainty and were therefore obliged to deal with many thorny problems, although they could not provide final solutions. Vinogradoff calls attention to the division of opinion among the glossators on the question whether custom overrides imperial legislation.⁴ According to one view, the people in the *lex regia* had transferred all their power and authority to the emperor. Custom therefore became subordinated to statute, and the latter could not be repealed even by disuse. From another point of view, popular custom was regarded as the survival of the law-making authority of the people, which would justify the modification of statutory law by custom. Into this difficult problem Vacarius, a distinguished glossator, delved until he reached the conclusion that legislation could not be abrogated by custom, unless the people should resume the imperial authority and power which they had previously transferred. Such dialectical exercises were never completed by the glossators, whose work had to be followed by prolonged study and writing by commentators before the Corpus Juris could be fitted to the needs of everyday life. The glossators assumed that Justinian was still alive and ruling. It is not therefore surprising that their work remained an academic tour de force which, although it removed uncertainty from the law, did not adapt the law to the practical requirements of the time.

The fourteenth century found lawyers ready to examine the great gloss of Accursius and to write commentaries designed to show how the Roman law might be applied in actual life. The time had arrived, they thought, when a national Italian law could be

³ P. Vinogradoff, *Roman Law in Medieval Europe* (London, 1909), p. 48.
⁴ *Ibid.*, p. 57.

built through correlating the Lombard statute law, the statutes of the Italian cities, and the canon law with the Roman law. Their aim was nothing less than the creation of a common law, supplementary to the statute law of the cities, which the courts must take into account in the administration of justice. To this great juristic enterprise the commentators, the most important of whom was Bartolus of Sassoferrato, dedicated their lives.[5]

Bartolus, who was not only a student and teacher of the law but also a public official, was always ready to illustrate a legal point by appealing to his own experience. In his *Tractatus Testimoniorum* he refers to the civil law as a body of wisdom, a science, and an art. The first category applies chiefly to theology and metaphysics, but it also includes the work of the jurist. Thus Bartolus considers jurisprudence to deal with the highest concerns of the human mind, although he subordinates this subject to theology. Science commonly refers to the natural sciences, but is applied to the law not only in the Digest but also in the writings of the medieval jurists. Finally, the study of the law is an art and was described as such by Ulpian in the opening sentences of the Digest.

The civil law to Bartolus meant a body of knowledge which included much more than is comprised within the modern notion of law. To him it was a branch of study which was not surpassed in dignity by any other, and which was superior to all, except theology. The rules of law are deeply embedded in a philosophy without an understanding of which the law is crude and often meaningless. In the opinion of Bartolus, the canon law was empty and imperfect without the civil law. So exalted a view of the civil law was naturally displeasing to the churchmen. Although Bartolus did not share the hostility to the canon law expressed by many medieval civilians, he believed that most problems of the time could be approached, and many of them solved, through the medium of the civil law. The amazing success of Bartolus lay in his ability to adapt the work of the glossators to the administration of justice

[5] The best account of Bartolus and his work in English is C. N. S. Woolf, *Bartolus of Sassoferrato* (Cambridge, 1913).

in the courts. His commentaries dominated the practice of the courts. In the countries where they were received, they actually enjoyed statutory authority. Although the commentators elaborated many ingenious and fruitful theories of law and politics, they remained essentially practitioners whose fundamental aim was to make the law which they found workable. The professional maxim that no one was a jurist who was not a Bartolist (*nemo jurista nisi sit Bartolista*), indicated the pre-eminence in his day of Bartolus and his school.

Jurisprudence gained from Bartolus and the commentators scientific precision, although it lost much of the spirit of contemplative reflection which had characterized the earlier Roman jurists. Realism was bought at too high a price. What had disappeared from the gaze of the Bartolists was the relationship between the civil law and the other phenomena of the social sciences. The civil law was a body of wisdom, or *civilis sapientia,* but it could not comprise the whole of human knowledge. Law when detached from the other social sciences rapidly becomes rigid and loses contact with the people it is intended to serve. It degenerates into a set of rules to be observed only by lawyers and judges in a game which they play for their own advantage.

The school which Alciat founded, and which at Bourges was headed by Cujas, attempted to repair the scholasticism of the commentators.[6] Borrowing from the new humanism of the Renaissance, the men at Bourges brought a new method to the study of the law. They were not satisfied to confine their attention to the recovered Corpus Juris but insisted upon going directly to the sources. New texts were discovered and old ones criticized. Historical investigations were undertaken on a large scale. "Without

---

[6] There is no work in English which describes adequately the school established at Bourges. See P. E. Viard, *André Alciat* (Paris, 1926); M. Berriat-Saint-Prix, *Histoire du droit Romain suivi de l'histoire de Cujas* (Paris, 1821); J. Flach, *Cujas, les glossateurs et bartolistes* (Paris, 1883). See also the splendid article by F. W. Maitland, "English Law and the Renaissance," which is reprinted in *Select Essays in Anglo-American Legal History*, 3 vol. (Boston, 1907), I, pp. 168–207.

history," declared Baudouin, one of the great teachers of the school, "jurisprudence is blind." This became an accepted maxim at Bourges as the humanities and the knowledge of antiquities and history were brought to the elucidation of the law. As a result of the work done at Bourges, jurisprudence was greatly enriched and brought into a closer relationship with the culture of the Renaissance.

The Netherlands at the end of the sixteenth century was eclipsing France as the center of juristic studies. This was not surprising, because the provinces at the mouth of the Rhine had become the cockpit in which the battle for freedom in continental Europe was fought. The expulsion of the Spaniards and the establishment of the new Dutch republic was accompanied by the release of currents of liberal thought which profoundly influenced both law and politics. Although it is customary to think of the Netherlands at this time as having produced Hugo Grotius, who laid the foundations of modern international law, there were other legal scholars who dealt with the subject of jurisprudence. Perhaps the greatest of these was Althusius.

Johannes Althusius was a German who taught law in the university at Herborn and spent the last thirty-four years of his life as magistrate in the town of Emden. Almost on the border of the Dutch republic, Althusius maintained the closest contacts with the scholars of his time. He was frequently called to the cities of the Netherlands as consultant or to lecture in the universities on the subject of jurisprudence. He is best known to modern students for his treatise on political theory,[7] but it should not be overlooked that Althusius was primarily a teacher and student of the law. His *Jurisprudentia Romana*, published in 1588, undertook to systematize the law to a degree not previously attained. In the preface to his book he invites the leading jurists of the time to free themselves from dependence upon earlier arrangements of the civil law and to embark upon new logical principles of organization. In part Al-

[7] *Politica Methodice Digesta of Johannes Althusius,* ed. Friedrich (Cambridge, Mass., 1932).

thusius relied upon the work done earlier in the century by Petrus Ramus, a dedicated opponent of scholasticism. But Ramus applied his method to limited areas of the law and was soon forgotten. Althusius was the first to apply what he called a natural logic to the construction of a legal system. The result was that Althusius enjoyed the approval by jurists of his work well into the eighteenth century.[8]

It was, however, in the work of Grotius that jurisprudence received its greatest contribution. This Dutch scholar did nothing less than separate the science of jurisprudence from theology and religion. His conception of natural law leads back to the Stoics and the jurists of the early Roman empire. The only system of law which he really knew and understood was that evolved by the Romans. But Grotius believed that the law of nature comprised a body of rules which man is able to discover for himself by the use of his reason. The patient efforts of medieval thinkers to reconcile the divine with the natural law he brushed aside and elaborated a theory of natural law which was entirely secular.[9]

At the same time, Grotius thought the law of nature to be closely connected with morality. The Protestant Revolt had given to morality an individualistic tinge which came to color the whole of Grotius' system. The theory of natural law became a doctrine of natural rights. The transformation involved more than a redefinition of terms. When the doctrine of natural rights became fully disclosed, it not only presented a foundation for law and politics but also formulated a theory of rights with which jurisprudence had to deal. Jurisprudence since the seventeenth century has been the study of rights and their correlative duties.

[8] O. von Gierke, *Development of Political Theory*, tr. Freyd (New York, 1939), Ch. III. This is an English translation of Gierke's famous monograph entitled *Johannes Althusius und die Entwicklung der naturrechtlichen Staatstheorien*, 4th ed. (Breslau, 1929).

[9] The *De jure belli ac pacis* of Grotius has been translated by F. W. Kelsey and is published as No. 3 of "The Classics of International Law" (Oxford, 1925).

Since a right is a protected interest, absolute within its orbit, it must be considered in relation to the duties which it imposes upon others who do not enjoy the right. Legal rights are those interests around which the law has thrown its protection and in behalf of which the state will exercise its power. When the state acts to protect a right it necessarily imposes duties upon those who may seek to infringe the right. A right *in rem* may be exercised, under certain conditions, against the whole world. A right *in personam* can exist only against a defined person, but the courts will protect this right continuously against violation by such person. When one contemplates the field of rights and duties it is readily seen that jurisprudence comprises a science that is vast at the same time that it is dignified.

Jurisprudence does not cover the whole field of human knowledge, as might be implied by the first part of Ulpian's definition. It does deal with the science of the just and the unjust, which is the second part of the same definition. But modern jurisprudence attempts to conduct this study of the just and the unjust by concentrating upon the analysis of rights. Rights are classified and the relativity of rights and duties is scrutinized. Fundamental juristic conceptions are considered in relation to legal systems, but it is not the function of jurisprudence to outline a system of law much less to analyze the branches of the law, such as contracts or torts, and to recite what each contains. This belongs to a different discipline; jurisprudence remains faithful to general principles.

Although there is but one science of jurisprudence, there are many methods by which it may be approached. In modern times there are four principal methods through which the study of the subject has been undertaken: the analytical, the historical, the comparative, and the sociological. These methods are not mutually exclusive and will often reach conclusions which are identical or at least supplementary. No method is perfect and much may be learned by following the different patterns of thought, even though they lead to the same or similar conclusions. The modern schools

11

of jurisprudence are described in terms of the method each follows.[10]

THE ANALYTICAL SCHOOL

The analytical school is identified with John Austin and the English Utilitarians. Its foundations were laid by Bentham at the close of the eighteenth century, but the methods and materials of its reasoning were developed in the nineteenth century by John Austin, who began his lectures at the University College of London in 1828.[11] These lectures were the first English attempt to deal systematically and critically with a fully developed system of law. Austin had studied in Germany the ancient and modern Roman law and brought to his knowledge of English law an acquaintance with the techniques of continental legal scholarship. His interest lay wholly with systems of law which were fully developed and his methods were peculiarly applicable to the study of law in quiet times.

Austin distinguishes at the outset between positive law and positive morality, and asserts the former to be the appropriate matter of jurisprudence. Following in the footsteps of Hobbes, he identifies law with command. The terms *command, duty,* and *sanction* are inseparably connected; each embraces the same ideas as the others, though each denotes those ideas in a particular series or order. In order to qualify as a law, a command must proceed from a political superior and be of such general character that it obliges a person or persons to a course of conduct. In other words, law implies not merely power controlling human action but also power controlling courses of human action. If an act be directed to a particular individual, it may very likely be an act of adminis-

[10] For an account of the schools of jurisprudence, see N. Isaacs, "Schools of Jurisprudence," *Harvard Law Review,* XXXI, pp. 373–411.

[11] J. Austin, *Lectures on Jurisprudence,* 5th ed. rev. and ed. by R. Campbell, 2 vol. (London, 1885). For comment on Austin, see E. C. Clark, *Practical Jurisprudence* (Cambridge, 1883) and W. J. Brown, *The Austinian Theory of Law* (London, 1906).

tration rather than of legislation. It assumes the form, though not the nature, of law.

Law, in the opinion of Austin, emanates from sovereign power. "Every positive law," he writes, "or every law simply and strictly so called, is set by a sovereign person, or a sovereign body of persons, to a member or members of the independent political society wherein that person or body is supreme. Or (changing the expression) it is set by a monarch, or sovereign number, to a person or persons in a state of subjection to its author. Even though it sprang directly from another fountain or source, it is a positive law, or a law strictly so called, by the institution of that present sovereign in the character of political superior." Thus Austin is brought to the necessity of defining sovereignty.[12]

Much criticism has been heaped upon Austin because of his theory of sovereignty. Undoubtedly he believed he was pursuing the line of thought begun by Bodin and Hobbes. Initially Bodin defined sovereignty as "supreme power over citizens and subjects unrestrained by laws." This bold definition he was unable to maintain, as he was obliged to recognize the existence of limitations upon sovereignty in the laws concerning the supreme power which the sovereign could not abrogate or modify. Moreover, Bodin was too closely bound by medieval thought to disregard the limitations of divine and natural law upon sovereign power.

Hobbes in his assertion that law is the command of the sovereign was more thoroughgoing than Bodin. Of course, he also was unable to deny the existence of divine and natural law as limitations upon sovereignty. But he ingeniously absorbed both divine and natural law in his definition of civil law. No rule could claim the quality of law unless it emanated from the sovereign. Thus civil law and natural law contain each other and the divine law can be made known to man only as it appears in the commands of the sovereign.

The absolutism of Hobbes did not succeed in establishing a place for itself in the English political system. The Revolution of 1688

[12] Austin, I, Lect. VI.

resulted in the recognition of sovereignty as vested in the king in Parliament. That is to say, sovereign power in England came to reside in the organs of government operating according to recognized rules. The personal rule of the king as practiced by the Stuarts was replaced by a constitutional monarchy. The supremacy of Parliament was proclaimed but this did not mean that government was arbitrary. Blackstone could write a half century later that "the power of Parliament is absolute and without control."[13] But all that this broad assertion could mean was that the statute-making power of Parliament was unrestricted.

Hobbes failed to recognize that the sovereign, although not limited in the power to make law, could be restricted in other ways. Government at best is only a delegation of power from the people. This might be effected by a conveyance in which all authority passed into the hands of the government without limitation, or it might be in the nature of a concession revocable upon conditions set forth in the transfer of power. Hobbes inclined toward the former view; but he could not, even in the time in which he lived, assert without fear of contradiction the political omnipotence of government. John Locke challenged the Hobbesian conception by declaring that the people delegated to government the power which it exercised in the nature of a trust. A breach of the trust gave rise to the reserve power of revolution through which the people might cashier their governors and delegate to other hands the powers of government. In this conception appears a distinction between the legal and the political sovereign.

The confusion which arose over the meaning of sovereignty was not resolved by Austin. His definition of sovereignty is well known.

If a determinate human superior, not in a habit of obedience to a like superior, receive habitual obedience from the bulk of a given society, that determinate superior is sovereign in that society, and the society (including the superior) is a society political and independent. To that

[13] W. Blackstone, *Commentaries on the Laws of England*, 2 vol. (Philadelphia, 1868), I, p. 160.

determinate superior the other members of the society are subject; or on that determinate superior, the other members of the society are dependent. The position of its other members towards that determinate superior, is a state of subjection, or a state of dependence. The mutual relation which subsists between that superior and them, may be styled the relation of sovereign and subject, or the relation of sovereignty and subjection.[14]

There is in this definition no clear distinction between legal and political sovereignty. Power and authority over others are recognized as attributes of sovereignty, but it is not clear that there is no exercise of sovereign power unless constitutional rules are observed. John Chipman Gray has pointed out this defect in the work of Austin. "Parliament, for instance," he wrote, "is said by Austin to be the Sovereign of England; but suppose, King, Lords, and Commons should meet in one chamber and vote together, an order passed by them would not be obeyed by the English people."[15] Parliament is not less restricted by modern constitutional usage than was Bodin's sovereign by the *leges imperii*, or laws concerning the supreme power.

Austin falls into real difficulty when he seeks to find the location of sovereignty in the United States. His broad definition of sovereignty in federal governments is that it "resides in the united governments as *forming one aggregate body*." He then proceeds to say of the United States:

I believe that the common government, or the government consisting of the Congress and the President of the United States, is merely a subject minister of the united states' governments. I believe that none of the latter is properly sovereign and supreme, even in the state or political society of which it is the immediate chief. And, lastly, I believe that the sovereignty of each of the states, and also of the larger state arising from the federal union, resides in the states governments as *forming one aggregate body*: meaning by a state's government, not its ordinary legislature, but the body of its citizens which appoints its ordinary legislature, and which, the union apart, is properly sovereign therein.

[14] Austin, I, pp. 220–1.
[15] J. C. Gray, *Nature and Sources of the Law* (New York, 1909), p. 74.

Of course, this application of Austin's definition of sovereignty would not be generally understood in the United States. The Constitution is a document of defined powers which apply to individuals only to a limited degree. If projected beyond the limits of the Constitution, governmental powers become a nullity.

Austin in a footnote attempts to surmount the difficulty by referring to the Fifth Article of the Constitution of the United States, which provides for amendments.[16] But the concurrent action of the parties necessary to the exercise of the amending power does not create a sovereign in Austin's sense. These are organs through which amendments are possible, provided the requirements of the Constitution are fulfilled. There still remains the distinction between sovereignty as the highest legal authority in the state and the actual power in the hands of the people.

Woodrow Wilson undertook to solve the problem by insisting that sovereignty is not identical with the powers of the community. "It is not," he said, "the general vitality of the organism, but the specific originative power of certain organs."[17] Correctly apprehending the meaning of Austin, Wilson pointed out that "the obedience of the subject has always limited the power of the sovereign." With obedience established as the correlative of sovereignty, it follows that sovereignty is the highest political power in the state, lodged in active organs, for the purpose of governing." This power must be distinguished carefully from the control lodged in the hands of the people. "Sovereign power is a positive thing," declared Wilson, "control a negative thing. Power belongs to government, is lodged in organs of initiative; control belongs to the community, is lodged with the voters. To call these two things by the same name is simply to impoverish language by making one word serve for a variety of meanings."[18]

The acuteness which Wilson displayed in his definition of sovereignty failed him when he undertook to point out in the govern-

16 Austin, I, pp. 257–63.
17 *An Old Master and Other Political Essays* (New York, 1893), p. 80.
18 *Ibid.*, p. 91.

ment of the United States the exact organs in which sovereignty is lodged. He was too much impressed with the importance of the States in the Union for his remarks to gain acceptance even at the time he wrote. The growth of federal centralization since that time has carried political thought still further from the position which he then assumed. For it was Wilson's belief that the members of the Union were genuine states, although their "sphere is limited by the presiding and sovereign powers of a state subordinated to them. . . . They have dominion; but it has sovereignty."[19] Certainly the decisions of the United States Supreme Court expanding national power have left little to the dominion of the states.

The failure of the Austinian conception of sovereignty to find universal application has led some writers to reject as unnecessary to jurisprudence the idea of a sovereign. Modern totalitarian forms of government readily admit drawing a precise line between sovereign and subjects, but elsewhere the distinction is difficult to maintain.

The idea of the State is fundamental in Jurisprudence, but having postulated the State, we can turn at once to see what are its organs, legislative, judicial, and administrative, and to consider the rules in accordance with which they act. Austin's method would be to attempt to discover the sovereign from the society, and then to refer the organs of government to the sovereign, but this intermediate step, which it is very difficult to take rightly, is superfluous. The organs of government can be as directly referred to the State as they can be to the sovereign.[20]

According to Gray, the real rulers of a political society are undiscoverable; they are the persons who dominate over the wills of their fellows. Nothing is therefore gained by introducing into jurisprudence a purely academic and unnecessary concept such as sovereignty.

The formidable attacks which have been made upon the work of Austin have not deterred other scholars from developing the ana-

[19] *Ibid.*, p. 94.   [20] Gray, pp. 76–7.

lytical method in the study of jurisprudence. The techniques need not be restricted to one system of law but they can hardly be extended beyond fully developed systems of law. No attention is paid to historical or sociological processes by which the law comes to exist. It is sufficient for the analytical jurist to consider the factual rules and materials which he finds in the legal system investigated by him.

Leadership of the analytical jurists was assumed by Holland, whose book first appeared in 1880.[21] Subsequently thirteen editions of the book were published, the last in 1924. The numerous and frequent revisions of the book call attention to a fundamental weakness in the analytical school. Whenever there are important changes in the English law, Holland finds revision of his book necessary. The same has been true of Salmond, whose elementary textbook began to compete with that of Holland in 1902.[22] Salmond's book by 1947 had gone through ten editions with substantial revisions in each reprinting. The law is progressive and is bound to change in order to adapt itself to new circumstances. A school of jurisprudence which depends largely upon logical deductions from the existing system of law can keep pace with legal changes only through frequent revisions of the materials of its reasoning. For this reason the analytical school of jurisprudence did its best work in the comfortable days of the nineteenth century.

Holland endeavored to define law in such a way as to avoid the complete reliance upon the sovereign found in Austin. "A law, in the proper sense of the term," he said, "is therefore a general rule of human action, taking cognizance only of external acts, enforced by a determinate authority, which authority is human, and, among human authorities, is that which is paramount in a political society." This definition Holland abbreviated to: "a general rule of external human action enforced by a sovereign political authority." While he steadfastly refused to recognize as laws any rules which could not reckon on the support of a sovereign political authority,

21 T. E. Holland, *The Elements of Jurisprudence*, 1st ed. (Oxford, 1880).
22 J. W. Salmond, *Jurisprudence*, 1st ed. (London, 1902).

he admits that: "there are states in which it is difficult to ascertain as a fact what rules answer to this description."[23]

Salmond performed two important services for analytical jurisprudence. In the first place, he defined law "as the body of principles recognized and applied by the state in the administration of justice." In the second place, he insisted that "all law is not made by the legislature. In England much of it is made by the law courts."[24] Thus the troublesome concept of sovereignty is subordinated to the power of the state at the same time that the courts are elevated to an equal position with the legislature in the creation of law. The rules made by the legislature are statute-law and those made by the courts are case-law. No conflict can arise in England, because an act of Parliament cannot be voided by the courts. In the United States an act of legislation can be annulled by the courts but only because it conflicts with the Constitution. Both the legislature and the courts are subordinated to the Constitution, which is the supreme law of the land.

In the work of Paton, one of the most recent writers of the analytical school of jurisprudence, the student is warned against the assumption that there is but one useful path for jurisprudence to tread. "Each," he said, "must work according to his own endowment, and individual preference will determine the issue." Instead of discovering universal rules of law, and creating a rigid scheme of classification into which all legal systems can be fitted, jurisprudence should attempt to discover as much as possible concerning legal method, to study the concepts of law and to trace the influence of social forces upon their development. "Jurisprudence," Paton remarked, "is not primarily interested in discovering uniformities, for diversity may be even more important."[25] But this discovery cannot be made solely through the logical deductions of analytical jurisprudence.

[23] Holland, 13th ed., Chs. II–IV.
[24] Salmond, 9th ed., p. 49.
[25] G. W. Paton, *A Textbook of Jurisprudence* (Oxford, 1946), p. 31.

The tendency to broaden the scope of jurisprudence to embrace all social science has been challenged in our own day by Hans Kelsen.[26] His works have been widely read in a number of languages, and his pure theory of law has resulted in much commentary. Kelsen maintains that the science of law should be divested of all non-legal elements. Neither history nor sociology can be said to have anything to do with jurisprudence.

Kelsen proposes to study legal rules abstracted from all social conditions. In order to do this he defines a hierarchy of norms in which each standard to be met will depend for its validity upon a superior norm. In the last analysis it is the state which imposes all legal rules. The legal order is the hierarchy of norms and the state is the legal order with fully developed institutions for the creation and enforcement of the law. Jurisprudence is the knowledge of these norms which comprise the legal order. The decision of a court to fine or imprison an individual for a violation of the law depends upon a superior norm which prescribes the course of conduct which has been violated. This in turn depends upon a superior norm which defines the form of government of the state. The norms become concrete as they approach the final norm which imposes an obligation upon a particular individual. They become less capable of recognition as they are traced backward to the fundamental norm which is identical with the political constitution of the country.

The theory of Kelsen is an interesting revival of the original foundations of the analytical school of jurisprudence. Austin in 1832 did much to rescue jurisprudence from the confusion of a vague mysticism. Kelsen has done something to banish fallacies from the study of law. But the science of law cannot stand apart from the other social sciences. Jurisprudence especially requires the co-operation of history and sociology if it is to explain the evolution of law.

[26] H. Kelsen, *General Theory of Law and State*, tr. Wedberg (Cambridge, Mass., 1949); *Reine rechtslehre* (Leipzig, 1934); See also W. Ebenstein, *The Pure Theory of Law* (Madison, Wis., 1945).

THE HISTORICAL SCHOOL

The historical school of jurisprudence examines the manner of growth of a legal system. It should be distinguished from legal history which is descriptive rather than critical. The function of historical jurisprudence is to interpret the changes which have taken place in the law and to estimate the forces which have produced those changes. Historical jurists have tended to regard custom as the foundation upon which the law was originally based. While they discarded the principle of natural law, they did not reject the advances based thereupon.[27] At the time they began their work, no other method appeared to promise more fruitful results than patient research into the past. The writings of the historical school must be consulted if we are to learn how the law came to arise and to develop.

The founder of the historical school of jurisprudence is said to be Savigny, although earlier jurists are entitled to some credit for their contributions. Indeed, the historical method applied to the study of law goes back at least to the time of Cujas and gains acceptance in the work of Hugo. In effect, the historical school was a reaction against the a priori methods of reasoning of the eighteenth century. Burke warned against constructing schemes for the future without pondering the lessons of the past. In his pamphlet, *On the Vocation of Our Age for Legislation and Jurisprudence*,[28] Savigny said: "In the earliest times to which authentic history extends, the law will be found to have already attained a fixed character, peculiar to the people, like their manners, language, and constitution. Nay, these phenomena have no separate existence, they are but the particular faculties and tendencies of an individual

---

[27] F. Berolzheimer, *The World's Legal Philosophies* (Boston, 1912), pp. 6-7, 204-15.

[28] The pamphlet was first published in 1814 at Tübingen under the title *Vom Beruf unserer Zeit für Gesetzgebung und Rechtswissenschaft.* An English translation by A. Hayward was published at London in 1831. See also H. Kantorowicz, "Savigny and the Historical School of Law," *Law Quarterly Review,* LIII, pp. 326-343.

people, inseparably united in nature, and only wearing the semblance of distinct attributes to our view. That which binds them into one whole is the common conviction of the people, the kindred consciousness of an inward necessity, excluding all notion of an accidental and arbitrary origin."[29]

Law, in the opinion of Savigny, is a spontaneous emanation from the life and spirit of a people. It is, like their language, customs, and songs, an expression of spiritual life which can be harmed by the clumsy intervention of legislation. Custom as a source of law in more advanced stages of civilization requires representation by jurists and must be made known through decisions of courts. Thus the judicial branch of the government becomes the agency through which the law is recognized.

Savigny was interested not only to postpone codification, which the work of Napoleon had made popular in Germany, but also to oppose the natural law school which had dominated the legal thinking for so long a time. The historical school emphasized the need for careful research into the monuments of the past. Savigny knew that if the history of Germany were investigated there would come to light a wealth of Germanic law which had been almost completely obscured since 1495.

The leading English exponent of the historical school was Sir Henry Maine. His theory that legal development has been a movement from status to contract is his most important contribution to legal theory. By this he means that there is a steady progression in society from a fixed condition in which the individual finds himself a part of a group to a social system based on contract. In the latter system the individual enjoys rights which flow from voluntary action and are the result of the exercise of the human will.[30]

Maine spent his life in the study of legal antiquities among which he found the early Roman law the most rewarding. He served the

[29] *On the Vocation*, etc., p. 24.
[30] H. J. S. Maine, *Ancient Law*, Everyman's Library ed. (London, 1931); *Dissertations on Early Law and Customs* (New York, 1886); *Lectures on the Early History of Institutions* (New York, 1875); *Village Communities in the East and West* (London, 1876).

British government in India from 1862 to 1869, where he studied carefully the institutions of the Indian people comparing them with more advanced societies. The method which he pursued has some definite disadvantages for the study of jurisprudence. It has a tendency toward reaction, to oppose changes in the law when it should be qualified to say what reforms should be made. Too many historians are inclined to spend their time trying to justify the past rather than to prescribe for the present and the future. At the same time it must be admitted that the historical school has saved some countries from making mistakes.

THE COMPARATIVE SCHOOL

The comparative school of jurisprudence is a recent expansion of the historical school. It seeks to apply the historical method to the study of two or more legal systems to discover their similarities and differences. The task set by this school has not been easy, because of the hostility between the civilians and the lawyers of the common law. Men trained in the Roman law have tended to despise the confusion and archaisms of English law, whereas the common lawyers, with the rich heritage which has come down to them from Bracton, Coke, and the reports of judicial decisions, have been almost smugly satisfied with the English system. Complacency among civilians as well as common lawyers has been rudely jolted by the comparative jurists as they have demonstrated that all the social sciences must be brought to serve the science of jurisprudence.

Actually the foundations of comparative jurisprudence are very old, extending back to the Bolognese glossators of the eleventh century. The methods which the Italians used were designed to illuminate comparative law. No great improvements have been made in their methods. Some criticism of the school has arisen because it does not take into account many systems of law, such as the Chinese, the Egyptian, and the Assyrian. This criticism is not very important, because the greater part of the world is under the English common law or some particular derivation of the Roman law. If the common law and the civil law be studied comparatively, a sufficient broad base will be found for the method. At the same time it must be admitted that the comparative school has done its best work within the field of legislation.

In the prosecution of his work, the student of comparative jurisprudence may strive to discover those legal rules which are common to the systems of law under examination or he may discuss the relations of individuals which have legal consequences and inquire how those relations find expression in the legal systems considered. The latter aspect of the study brings comparative jurisprudence into close touch with anthropology, philology, sociology, and the biological sciences. Indeed, it was the Darwinian theory in the field of biology that furnished a guide to all studies of organic evolution. A large and diversified group may therefore claim credit for the founding of the comparative school, in which appear among the jurists Frederick William Maitland, Sir Frederick Pollock, and Sir Paul Vinogradoff.[31]

THE SOCIOLOGICAL SCHOOL

Although the sociological school of jurisprudence owes its origin to the Austrian Gumplowicz, it has had its greatest success in the United States. Perhaps it is a mistake to regard the sociological as a fully matured school for the study of law. It should be more correct to describe it as a school in the process of development. Only the future will determine how far the work of the school will shape the course of jurisprudence. In any event, the sociological school

[31] F. W. Maitland, *Select Passages from the Works of Bracton and Azo* (London, 1895); *Bracton's Note Book* (London 1887).

F. Pollock, *Essays in Jurisprudence and Ethics* (London, 1882); *Essays in the Law* (London, 1922); *Expansion of the Common Law* (London, 1922); *A First Book of Jurisprudence* (New York, 1896); *The Genius of the Common Law* (New York, 1912).

P. Vinogradoff, *Collected Papers*, 2 vol. (Oxford, 1928); *Common-sense in Law* (New York, 1914); *Custom and Right* (Cambridge, Mass., 1925); *Outlines of Historical Jurisprudence*, 2 vol. (Oxford, 1920–22); *Roman Law in Medieval Europe* (London, 1909).

has already served a valuable purpose in opposing the extreme reliance of the analytical jurists upon logic as a tool in the study of the law.

Gumplowicz was a Polish Jew who viewed all social phenomena as an unending struggle between different elements: first between racial groups, then between the states formed by the stronger groups, and finally between the classes within these states. Law is one of the most important instruments by which the stronger group within the state attains its objectives. Law, according to Gumplowicz, is dominion by the strong and the few over the many and the weak, and as such is a necessary expression of inequality and social differentiation. In other words, the Gumplowicz theory of law is directly opposed to the natural law theory in which equality before the law is a major premise. Gumplowicz scoffed at natural law as a preposterous product of the imagination.[32]

If this were all that Gumplowicz said we could dismiss his thesis as a pure power theory of the law. But he observed in history that law has been used by the underprivileged classes to overthrow the dominion of the ruling class. Every class that has been excluded from power relies upon law to gain the mastery over the rulers and to obtain rulership for itself. Thus law is an important factor in the emancipatory struggles of the human race. What Gumplowicz failed to recognize was that law assumes different forms in different stages of society. In earlier societies law does not achieve either freedom or equality but in the higher and more developed forms of the law some sphere of freedom is assigned to each citizen, and at least a formal equality of all citizens before the law is guaranteed.

In crossing the Atlantic the sociological school of jurisprudence met new ideas which greatly modified its teaching. William James, the great psychologist, had at the end of the nineteenth century opposed the dominant rationalism of his time with an empirical

[32] L. Gumplowicz, *The Outlines of Sociology*, tr. Moore (Philadelphia, 1899).

study of human experience. James took exuberant delight in attacking the philosophy of natural law which had so long dominated American political and legal thinking. Law, he said, was to be judged not by the application of eternal standards or reason, but by experimental methods. There is a pragmatic approach to the study of law which applies the test of whether a rule will work. Jurisprudence becomes a science of social engineering.

Leadership among American jurists of the sociological school must be given to Roscoe Pound, for many years Dean of the Harvard Law School. The legal order, said Pound, is not primarily concerned with rights. It is concerned with interests, claims, and demands. A right is merely one among various means for the satisfaction of interests. In the past people have written about law as a record of increasing recognition of individual rights, but it is just as easy to regard the history of law as a wider recognition of social interests. Pound thinks of law as a maximum satisfaction of wants, not as a maximum of self-assertion.[33]

The sociological school is at once a reaction against the analytical jurists and a protest against the doctrine of natural law. Justice is not to be attained through blind obedience to some supposed higher law but by patient experimentation with the materials of human existence. The men who hold this philosophy of jurisprudence are in full agreement with Justice Oliver Wendell Holmes, who said:

The life of the law has not been logic; it has been experience. The felt necessities of the time, the prevalent moral and political theories, intuitions of public policy, avowed or unconscious, even the prejudices which judges share with their fellow-men, have had a good deal more to do than the syllogism in determining the rules by which men should be governed. The law embodies the story of a nation's development through many centuries, and it cannot be dealt with as if it contained only the axioms and corollaries of a book of mathematics. In order to know what it is, we must know what it has been, and what it tends to

[33] R. Pound, *Interpretations of Legal History* (New York, 1923); *An Introduction to the Philosophy of Law* (New Haven, 1925); *Law and Morals*, 2nd ed. (London, 1926); *Spirit of the Common Law* (Francestown, N.H., 1947).

become. We must alternately consult history and existing theories of legislation. But the most difficult labor will be to understand the combination of the two into new products at every stage.[34]

Only the judge or lawyer who is acquainted with the more remote and more general aspects of the law, said Holmes, will be in a position to fulfill his social functions properly.

All schools of jurisprudence have contributed something to the development of the law. The analytical jurists reclaimed the subject from the chaos in which Austin found it. By the power of logical analysis much dead wood was cleared away. Austin and his followers, however, tied the law to the existence of a sovereign who could not always be found. The result has been that analytical jurisprudence has done its best work in the field of definition. It has coldly dissected the law as it existed in the nineteenth century, but it has done little to further its development.

The historians have done a great deal to prevent people from making the same mistakes that were made in the past. History serves its highest purpose in satisfying curiosity. But once a knowledge of the past has been achieved, it becomes important that its lessons be used to guard against mistakes in the present and future. The weakness of the historical school of jurisprudence is that it has tried too hard to justify the past and in so doing has glossed over the mistakes. People keep on doing the things they should not do because the teaching of history is not recognized or followed.

The comparative jurists have to their credit important advances in the technical study of the law. We are indebted to the Italian glossators for the method of legal study through parallel passages and the making of indices in legal studies begun by them. In modern times comparative jurisprudence has increased our knowledge of the civil law as well as the common law at the same time that it has pointed out the similarities and the differences in the two systems. But like the historians, the work of the comparative jurists is only a starting point for jurists who wish to improve the law.

[34] O. W. Holmes, Jr., *The Common Law* (Boston, 1881), p. 1.

Finally, the sociological school of jurisprudence opens up unlimited possibilities to develop the law in keeping with human experience. The law must be studied as a part of the whole field of social science. Perhaps in time the method which these men have adopted will become the most rewarding for the study of the law.

II

The Meaning of Justice

JUSTICE IS PERHAPS the most enduring concept in legal and political thought. The *Republic* of Plato is commonly believed to be a study of justice; certainly this book dominated Greek thinking and its influence has continued throughout the western world to the present time.[1] But justice to Plato meant something very different from what it has meant to medieval and modern writers. At the outset, Plato rejects the legalistic view that "justice is the giving to each man what is proper to him," a view which was later to become the basis of Ulpian's definition. He also condemns as vicious the Sophist definition "that justice is nothing else than the interest of the stronger." Plato's doctrine is that justice is a part of human virtue and is therefore synonymous with morality.

Today we think of justice and injustice in relation to judicial and administrative acts. A judge who metes out the proper punishment for theft is a just judge, but we would not speak of the thief as unjust. In Plato's thought a thief is an unjust man because he has departed from the virtue which entitles him to be called good.

[1] *Dialogues of Plato*. tr. Jowett, 2 vol. (New York, 1937), I, 591–897.

Human virtues culminate in justice, which is the quality of self-restraint. Every man, if he is to attain virtue, must exercise his talents for the good of himself and his fellow men, but this exercise must be carried out with restraint. No man develops character and personality by throwing his weight around. Plato takes for granted that there is nothing unsocial or antisocial in well-bred human beings which might result in disharmony precisely because of a complete and perfect development of individual powers. This assumption is not obviously true, and many writers have questioned it, but Plato was always certain that he was correct. It never occurred to him that socialized training might be repressive of self-expression. He always believed that the individual who was seeking to develop his own powers, but who at the same time paid sympathetic heed to the aspirations of other men, was a just man.

Plato then makes the assumption that the state is merely the individual "writ large." Justice is at once a part of human virtue and the bond which joins men together in society. It is an identical quality which makes man good and which makes him social. Plato holds that the rules which make society possible are identical with the rules which make men good. The task of the ruler is on the one hand to maintain the organization of society, and on the other to perfect the nature of the citizens. These are not two tasks, but two aspects of the same task; rulership and education must go together.

The real service performed by Plato in the *Republic* is his demonstration that justice cannot be defined merely as obedience to law. It is a crude definition of justice which identifies just conduct with conduct in conformity with law. Justice is obedience to law, provided law is understood to be that which binds men together in political association. It cannot be limited to the law of the land, which embraces what is socially expedient whether or not it is morally right.

ROMAN DEFINITIONS OF JUSTICE

The identification of law and justice is the accomplishment of Cicero, who saw in nature the test of truth and validity in law, in social order, and in civil society. To live according to nature, he said, is the highest good. Cicero was not a philosopher but a lawyer who spent most of his time in client caretaking. He did not refine his ideas but set forth in his speeches and essays what right-minded Romans of his time were thinking.

The new notion which one finds in the work of Cicero is that of natural law.[2] Borrowed from Stoic philosophy, it is the idea that there is a single law or system of laws governing the entire universe, to which all natural things have an obligation to conform. "True law," he said, "is right reason in agreement with nature; it is of universal application, unchanging and everlasting; it summons to duty by its commands, and averts from wrongdoing by its prohibitions." Inanimate things are bound to obey this law by natural necessity, but man discovers the law of nature through his reason. "For those creatures who have received the gift of reason from nature," Cicero remarks, "have also received right reason, and therefore they have also received the gift of law, which is right reason applied to command and prohibition. And if they have received law, they have received justice also. Now, all men have received reason; therefore all men have received justice."

It was clear to Cicero that the civil law is organically related to the ultimate law of reason and justice and is not merely the expression of the capricious will of the lawgiver. There was no place in the Roman law for the whimsical utterance of the ruler whom Juvenal quotes as saying: "*Sic volo, sic jubeo, sic pro ratione voluntas.*" Human commands can never serve in place of reason; they must be the product of reason. Human laws, whether in the form of *ius civile* or *ius gentium*, must harmonize with the law of nature, which is the final source of all law.

[2] R. W. and A. J. Carlyle, *History of Medieval Political Theory*, 6 vol. (London, 1903–36), I, Ch. 1.

In the theory of Cicero all men are equal in their capacity to discern the natural law. For him, the natural law is actual law existing throughout the universe and in subordination to which all human rules must be made. Behind all actual laws and customs of men there exists a supreme and permanent law, to which all human order, if it is to have any truth or validity, must conform. This is the law of nature.

It should not be forgotten that Aristotle in one passage of the *Nichomachean Ethics* propounded a doctrine of natural law.[3] But for the Greek there is a natural inequality among men which makes impossible a theory of the state in which nature gives law and justice to every man who will receive them. Man is by nature a social and political animal, according to ancient Greek thought, but men are divided by nature in respect of their capacities for virtue. Some will be freemen and others slaves. Men are no more equal than they are of one size. Aristotle was doubtless thinking of nature as distributing benefits to mankind in unequal portions which find reflections in the different constitutions of states. But there will always be one constitution which is better than others because it approaches the ideal which is nature's plan. "The rules of justice," he says, "which are not natural, but human, are not everywhere identical, but everywhere there is one constitution only marked out by nature as the best." The task of mankind is therefore one of constitutional construction in which human wisdom seeks to achieve the model of what law ought to be, and what it may become if men are wise enough to penetrate the mystery of nature.

The Roman lawyers, who followed Cicero in the second and third centuries of the Christian era, did not dwell at length on the meaning of justice. Ulpian, it is true, defined justice as "the fixed and perpetual will to give to everyone his due." This definition was repeated constantly throughout the Middle Ages and was set forth in the Corpus Juris. Justice was regarded at all times as a quality

[3] Book V, Ch. 7.

of will or purpose. But it was not until the rise of the Church Fathers that justice became identified with the will of God.

THE CHURCH FATHERS AND JUSTICE

The Church Fathers, as the group of early Christian writers is called, embraced a large number of men from St. Clement of Rome and the Twelve Apostles in the first century to St. Isidore of Seville in the seventh century. These men were Romans at the same time that they were Christians, and it is to be expected that much of their work would be in the traditional currents of thought which swept through the Roman Empire of their day. Although the chief source of their thought was the Bible, some of them were tutored in the Roman law and the secular literature of Rome. Indeed, until recently our only knowledge of some of the work of Cicero was what could be gleaned from quotations from his books by Lactantius and St. Augustine. One will seek in vain in the writings of the Church Fathers for a systematic treatment of the state and its institutions, but many of them dealt with the leading concepts of legal and political theory.

St. Augustine, whose active life came at the close of the fourth century and the beginning of the fifth century, was the most important of the Church Fathers. His life was spent largely in the town of Hippo in north Africa, where he became a bishop and struggled to advance the Christian religion. It was here that he wrote his *City of God*, in which he restates from the Christian point of view the ancient idea that man is a citizen of two cities, the city of his birth and the city of God. The religious meaning of this distinction had already been suggested by Seneca and Marcus Aurelius. Man's nature is twofold; he is spirit and body, and therefore at once a citizen of this world and of the heavenly city. The fundamental fact of human life is the division of human interests, the worldly interests that center about the body and the other-worldly interests that belong specifically to the soul. This distinction is basic in all Christian thought on ethics and politics and finds expression in gospel hymns today.

Justice in the thought of St. Augustine is incomplete, if it is not based upon Christian law as well as the law of nature.[4] He criticizes the definition of justice given by Cicero so severely that some writers have suggested that St. Augustine dispensed with the need of justice in a commonwealth. What St. Augustine undoubtedly meant was that justice, while essential to bind a people together in a state, cannot be wholly achieved where the people do not worship the true God. It is important in this connection to note the practical end which St. Augustine had in view of extending the teachings of the Christian faith within his diocese. He prudently refrained from denying any merit to pagan states, but he reserved the recognition of justice as rendering to each his due to states whose people were Christians.

The importance of St. Augustine's definition of justice lies in the conception of a single universal order which transcends the state. Both Plato and St. Augustine regarded justice as conformity to order; a society which did not maintain order through rules of law was inconceivable to the Greek as well as to the Christian. But Plato conceived man to belong to no society wider than the state, and subject to no law beyond that of the state. To him the individual achieves justice when he takes his proper place in society. A just man will fulfill his appointed purpose when he conforms to the rules of the state of which he is a member. St. Augustine, on the other hand, saw man as a member of a universal and eternal society and subject to its universal and eternal law. Plato's standard of justice was limited to a social order which could change or pass away. The law which is the standard of justice according to St. Augustine is the same for all times and for all men. Hence justice for him was measured by an absolute standard.

St. Augustine is also able to apply his standard of justice to the acts of states. In the same way that a man can be unjust in trans-

[4] *Basic Writings of St. Augustine,* ed. W. J. Oates. 2 vol. (New York, 1948).

gressing the law of a state, so also can a state commit injustice by the transgression of the law of God. With the greatest courage, St. Augustine rebukes the pagan emperors who had persecuted the early Christians. "What justice is that, then," he said, "which takes man from the true God, and gives him unto the condemned fiends?" The notion of an absolute standard of justice residing in the universal and eternal law of God held sway in the Middle Ages until it was modified by the reasonable interpretation of St. Thomas Aquinas. The whole theory of papal imperialism was founded upon the notion that justice must have as its basis the law of a Christian God.

In the interval between St. Augustine and St. Thomas Aquinas lies a period of eight hundred years during which men relied upon the heritage of the past for their notions of justice. From the feudal system they deduced certain principles of social order from the personal obligations of lord and vassal. But even here, the principle which lies behind every form of political authority is the principle of justice. As expressed by a phrase of the Assizes of the Court of Burgesses of Jerusalem, the authority of the lady or lord is only to do law or justice; they have no authority to behave unjustly.

THE LAWYERS AND JUSTICE

Law among the Teutonic peoples was never considered to come from the ruler. The king was in no sense sovereign. He could not make law, but was himself bound by it. The source of law was the customs of the people. When Bracton came to write his famous treatise, he was so unclear as to the dividing line between law and custom that he gave to his work the title *Laws and Customs of the English*. Both kings and people were subject to a law which neither made, and which assigned to each rank and class within the state its functions, duties, and rights. It was the function of the king to discover this law and to effect its promulgation, but he was in no sense its author and in no case could he override the law.

In the Teutonic tribes, and among the peoples of northern Eu-

35

rope generally, law was personal rather than territorial. That is to say, each individual was entitled to have his personal rights determined according to the law of his people. A Salian Frank took his inheritance according to the *Lex Salica,* whereas his Roman neighbor in a similar case was governed by the "Sententiae" of Paulus as reported in the Corpus Juris Civilis. This multiplicity of legal rules operating within a single jurisdiction might appear to the modern world to be chaotic. But to the people of the Middle Ages it was not confusing because they regarded the end of all law as the attainment of justice.

The churchmen throughout the early Middle Ages, St. Augustine excepted, did little to develop the meaning of justice. The spread of Christianity throughout western Europe "was accompanied by a rapid decline in the study of classical letters. Learning, such as it was, became restricted to the clergy and the monks, and these became more and more inclined to elevate their professional study at the expense, or to the condemnation, of every other."[5] Gregory the Great, who employed his unrivaled authority to denounce all secular learning, established the doctrine of the absolute and irresponsible authority of the ruler as the representative of God. According to this doctrine, the ruler was not only the source of law but was also normally not bound by the law. But this meant little more than the theory that the ruler was *legibus solutus* and there existed no court of justice before which he could be held accountable. Although the teachings of Gregory the Great persisted into the later Middle Ages, they did little to help man realize the principle of justice. The perfection of divine justice was an unattainable ideal which men might revere but which remained beyond their power to achieve. But the assertion of divine rulership of the world proved congenial to the clergy, and Cassiodoris insisted that the ruler is God's minister to secure justice. It was only one step to identify justice with the will of God.

This step the lawyers were obliged to take if they were to re-

[5] R. L. Poole, *Illustrations of Medieval Thought and Learning,* rev. ed. (London, 1920), p. 5.

concile divergent views regarding the nature and sources of the law. At no time during the Middle Ages did law schools cease to exist or systematic study of the Roman law die out in western Europe. The great law school at Bologna began to flourish in the eleventh century, but there were other and earlier schools in Italy and probably in southern France. Fragments of legal literature produced in these schools have been discovered which indicate a great deal of activity anterior to or at least independent of the school at Bologna.

Before the time of Irnerius and the great law school at Bologna, medieval lawyers had accepted the principle that justice is primarily a quality of God's will. At the hands of the great civilians of Bologna the ideas which had long been current were given more formal statement. Through the definition of terms, the civilians reached the conclusion that justice is primarily a quality of the will of God and secondarily that of man. "Neither God's will nor man's determines the nature of justice, but justice is the conformity of the will of God and man with that which is *aequum*, the conformity of the will of God with that which is His own nature."[6] The meaning is not very clear and indicates that the lawyers were groping for the solution of a practical problem which confronted them.

The problem to which a practical solution was sought was the reconciliation of the idea in the Roman law of the source of political authority with that pronounced by the clergy. The Roman lawyers had asserted that rulership is derived from the people and transferred to the ruler in the *lex regia*. At the same time, there grew up the idea encouraged by the Church Fathers that all authority sprang from God. In other words, there was an element in rulership which could not come from popular consent. It therefore followed that the Church had an important role in the elevation of the ruler to the throne. The consecration of the ruler was "associated with visible rites of a definitely ceremonial character. When, therefore, the Church sanctified a ruler's office by its con-

[6] Carlyle, II, pp. 9–11.

firmation it was natural that it should express its blessing in a formal legal act which symbolized the divine legitimation and endorsement of the right to the throne." The secular foundations of government were not thereby abandoned, but the ruler who had been anointed by the grace of God was at least strengthened in his material rights. "Once consecration was introduced, earthly authority was readily assimilated with the heavenly," and civil disobedience came to be regarded as sinful.[7]

The third element which had to be considered was the Teutonic notion of law as custom. As we have already seen, law to the Teutonic peoples was the customary law of the realm. Its enforcement rested with the popular courts. But the purpose of the state, according to the Church Fathers, was the enforcement not of the traditional law but the law of God or of nature as revealing the will of God. Hence clerical thought throughout the Middle Ages continued to regard the ruler as bound to observe the divine law and to be relieved of his subjection to customary law. But "Germanic and ecclesiastical opinion were firmly agreed on the principle, which met with no opposition until the age of Machiavelli, that the state exists for the realization of the law," and nobody dissented from the view that the purpose of the law is the maintenance of justice.[8]

The development of legal and political theory in the early Middle Ages was not systematic or scientific. The idea of a higher law derived either from God or nature prevailed. In subordination to the higher law the actual rules for the guidance of men were made. The purpose of law was everywhere said to be to enable the ruler to do justice. There might be controversies over the form law should take, but there was no doubt about its purpose. To the medieval mind the law was the practical form of justice, and it was in the maintenance of law that men found the security for justice and for all good in life. There is an excellent statement of the

[7] F. Kern, *Kingship and Law in the Middle Ages* (Oxford, 1939), pp. 40, 57.
[8] *Ibid.*, p. 70.

medieval notion in one of the Norman law books. The author looks upon law as created in order to restrain man's unbridled desires and the conflicts which these would cause if unchecked; it is God, the lover of justice, who has created princes in order that they may restrain the discord of men by definite laws.

Although civil society was in accordance with the will of God, few men in the Middle Ages said that God ordained any particular form of government, and there were fewer who said that God established any man as ruler. The theory which in a later period was to become the divine right of kings was known but not generally held in the Middle Ages. The medieval theory subscribed to the idea found in the Digest that the source of political authority is in the people.

If there is any lesson to be learned from the Middle Ages, it is that justice may be approached from many avenues. Nobody could define justice except in terms of some measure of law, but there existed a free, competitive market among legal rules. Of course, in time, as in the case with all free competition, some legal rules and legal systems ceased to flourish and were replaced or absorbed by other and more vigorous systems of law. The recovery of Roman law by the Bolognese glossators in the twelfth century resulted in the Corpus Juris of Justinian becoming the foundation of modern civil law on the continent of Europe. At the same time, in England, the king's justices, overriding local customs, built up a law common to the whole country. But neither the civil law on the continent nor the common law in England were less instruments for the achievement of justice than the laws and customs which they replaced, and in many cases out of which they were forged.

THE GREAT CONTRIBUTION OF
ST. THOMAS AQUINAS

Medieval discussions of the meaning of law culminated in the work of St. Thomas Aquinas. Writing in the thirteenth century, after the recovery of Aristotelian learning, St. Thomas sought nothing less than the reconciliation of the *Politics* of Aristotle with Christian dogma. His assertion that *gratia non tollit naturam, sed perfecit* placed St. Thomas in a position where he had to deviate from the teachings of the earlier churchmen. If grace does not abolish nature, but perfects it, human institutions could no longer be regarded as necessitated by sin. An essentially human standard of justice which is neither vitiated by sin nor absorbed in the absolute perfection of divine justice became possible.[9]

"Law," said St. Thomas, "is nothing but a dictate of the practical reason in a ruler who governs a complete community." Law is a rule or measure of action which must proceed from reason. It cannot spring from the whim or caprice of a ruler or be the product of tyranny and usurpation. The proper character of law is to command and to forbid; but to command belongs to reason, therefore law is a thing related to reason. It is reason which enables men to distinguish between order and anarchy in society.

It is equally important that the promulgation of law proceed from the whole community or from the political person whose duty is the care of the common good. A private person has no authority to compel right living. Hence St. Thomas is never concerned to establish the rights of the individual.

St. Thomas proceeds to define the various forms of law, giving first place to the eternal law as the divine plan of the universe. Since the world is governed by divine providence, it is clear that the whole universe is governed by divine reason, which has itself the nature of law.

The natural law is different from but related to the eternal law. Since all things which are under divine direction are subjected to rule and measure by the eternal law, it is manifest that all things participate in some manner in the eternal law. But rational crea-

[9] A collection of extracts from the writings of St. Thomas Aquinas, with Latin text and English translation, has been published by A. P. D'Entrèves, *Aquinas, Selected Political Writings* (Oxford, 1948). For a larger collection of the writings of St. Thomas, see *Basic Writings of St. Thomas*, 2 vol. Ed. A. C. Pegis (New York, 1945).

tures are subject to divine direction in a manner superior to that of all other creatures, since they can direct themselves and others and thus become themselves sharers in the directive activity. The rational creature has thus itself a share in the eternal reason and derives from this its natural inclination toward its proper action and end; and this manner of sharing in the eternal law, which is peculiar to the rational creature, is called the natural law. In other words, natural law is a bridge thrown across the gulf which divides man from God. In natural law is expressed the dignity and power of man, and thus of his reason, whereby he may participate intellectually and actively in the rational order of the universe. All men, through the illumination of God, have knowledge of the great principles of natural law and a natural inclination to observe them. But as principles they cannot be applied to specific cases unless he who has the care of a community makes them known in the form of human positive laws.

Human law is devised by men for the particular and detailed regulation of what the natural law ordains. It is necessary for the discipline of man, but it depends for its validity upon justice. Humanly enacted laws are in accord with reason to the extent that they are derived from that natural law. They include the *ius gentium*, a body of laws without which men could not live together, and the *ius civile*, which any state establishes as being suitable to its own conditions. But these particular rules, although deduced by human reason, have their source in nature.

St. Thomas admits that the human reason is not able to share to the full in the dictates of the divine reason, but only according to the measure of its own imperfect nature. But there are limits beyond which man may not go. Human laws must be for the common good and they must be promulgated by the person or persons who have the care of the whole community. A clear distinction must be maintained between king and tyrant; the rules of the latter are not laws but perversions of law, they are acts of violence rather than laws. To the thorny question who is to pronounce judgment on a tyrant and what is to be done with him, St. Thomas has no more practical answer than other believers in passive obedience. Ridding the people of a tyrant must be undertaken by lawful means.

Finally, the term *divine law* is used by St. Thomas to describe the twofold law of God which is revealed in the Old and New Testaments. Because man is destined for the end of eternal blessedness, which exceeds the measure of human faculties, he should be guided toward his end by a law given by God. For other reasons, such as the uncertainty of men's reason, the inability of human laws to deal with the inward acts, which are hidden, and the certainty that attempts by men to punish or prevent all bad acts would do more harm than good, the divine law is needed. The divine law does not contradict or annul the natural law, but was added so that man might participate in the eternal law *altioro modo*.

Law in all its forms is the expression of reason but, according to St. Thomas, it is also the expression of justice. Ulpian had defined justice as the fixed and perpetual will to give to everyone his right, a definition which St. Thomas accepts with the proviso that it be correctly understood. In order to make clear his understanding of justice, St. Thomas embarks upon a discussion of the judicial process wherein he seeks to explain what Aristotle meant when he said that men go to the judge as to a living justice. Written human laws are fully recognized as a source of rights and justice. But they derive their force not from being but from nature itself. Human laws which are contrary to the natural law are unjust and have no force. Therefore, according to St. Thomas, the judge in seeking to do justice may sometimes have to look beyond the written law to the equity which the legislator desired to attain.

St. Thomas regarded all law as founded upon reason for the purpose of achieving justice. In this respect he deviated from the churchmen who preceded him and from the feudal lawyers. His reading of Aristotle's *Politics* taught him that law was neither the custom of the people nor the will of the ruler. Neither could law be confined to the word of God. Undoubtedly God ordained the state, but only because the state was natural to man. In the unending quest for justice man was to utilize his reason not only to attain the salvation of his soul but also to promote peace and order on earth necessary to his happiness.

SIXTEENTH-CENTURY IDEAS OF JUSTICE

The quest for the meaning of justice was resumed in the sixteenth century during the French wars of religion touched off by the massacre of Protestants on the eve of St. Bartholomew's Day, 1572. There followed a tremendous amount of pamphleteering; all parties were eager to be heard in the controversy. Partisans ransacked the storehouse of accumulated legal and political theory to support their respective claims. Although these men stood on the threshold of the modern state, they wrote always in the shadow of medieval thought.

The Huguenots comprised the leading party among the French Protestants. They were the "sappers and miners" of the day whose decentralizing tendencies aimed at the subversion of the monarchy painfully constructed by the Counts of Paris. Their theory of politics was set forth in the *Vindiciae Contra Tyrannos*, which furnished a powerful medium for political thinking long after the Huguenot party had succumbed to the centralizing tendencies of Bourbon absolutism.[10]

According to the *Vindiciae Contra Tyrannos*, kingship is ordained by God, but it is the people who "establish kings, put the scepter into their hands, and who with their suffrages approve the election." Between God, the king, and the people, there is a covenant for the maintenance of the true religion. There is also a covenant "between the king and the people, that the people shall obey faithfully, and the king to command justly." This contract is made in subordination to the law of nature, which "teaches and commands us to maintain and defend our lives and liberties." There-

[10] A reprint of this book with an introduction by H. J. Laski was published under the title of *Liberty Against Tyrants* (London, 1924).

fore, any violation of the contract by the king is tyranny and may be resisted by the people.

Before this pamphlet had fallen from the press, George Buchanan, from his scrutiny of Scottish law and history, was composing his great dialogue to justify the deposition of Mary, Queen of Scots.[11] This famous treatise not only adopts the theory of contract but also finds the source of human association in a "certain innate propensity, not only in men but also in other animals of the gentler tribes, to associate readily, even without the allurements of utility, with beings of their species." Buchanan thinks they are to be reckoned citizens "who obey the laws and uphold the social compact, who choose rather to undergo all labors and dangers for the common safety than dishonorably to grow old in ease and sloth." Between the king and his subjects a contract exists; he who deviates from the contract dissolves it, and any rights which he may have enjoyed thereunder are forfeited. Thus Buchanan brought very near to England the compact philosophy and fixed the doctrine by which the Scottish nation organized itself against the king in the famous covenant of 1638.

It is important to note that the Scotchman recognized "utility as one cause, but not as the absolute mother of justice and equity, as some would have her; but rather as their handmaid, and one of the guardians of a well-regulated community." The fundamental impulse to social life springs from nature, which is "the light infused into our minds by the divinity." Similarly, the separatists of post-Reformation England were not steeped in the utilitarianism of today; they were able to pursue the idea of right beyond mere utility. "Is this so strange to John Robinson?" wrote a contemporary opponent of the Pilgrims. "Do we not know the beginnings of his church? That there was first one stood up and made a covenant, and then another, and these two joined together, and so a third, and these became a church, say they." In this undoubtedly true account of the formation of the Scrooby-Austerfield

[11] G. Buchanan, *De jure regni apud Scotos*. Eng. tr. (London, 1689). The references are to the English edition of 1721.

congregation is discovered a belief that in agreement consecrated by God is found a rule for human conduct.

Across the North Sea in The Netherlands toward the end of the sixteenth century a bitter war was waged in which the forces of Philip II of Spain were expelled from the country. The intensity of the religious differences was reflected in every aspect of the struggle. When peace was restored and the independence of the Dutch had been proclaimed, it remained for a Calvinist, Johannes Althusius, to state systematically the principles of the movement.

The *Politica Methodice Digesta*[12] of Althusius was first published in 1603, but was subjected to revision and reprinted in 1610. According to Althusius, the contract upon which civil government is founded is social; it is the mutual agreement of all to live in an ordered society. The efficient cause of political association is consent and the mutual agreement of the citizens joined together; the final cause is convenience, happiness, and common defense.

Society is composed of social groups raised by a continuous progression from private to public relationships. That is to say, there is in Althusius a federalistic idea which displays the state as entirely built up on the principle of association. At the bottom are presented the natural functions and relations such as arise out of marital relationships and family organization. From these come the civil relationships, born of wills which have united and created, in the human life, artificial groups for the utility of many. Examples of the latter are colleges, cities, provinces, and empires. But the principle of association is always the same; it is that of contract. The system of Althusius is admirably adapted to support his definition of politics, which is the art of joining men together for the establishment, the direction, and the preservation of the social life.

Although poles apart from the Calvinism of Althusius, the Jesuits held a theory of the state which is similar in many respects to that of the German jurist. To the Jesuits the state is of secular

---

[12] A modern edition of this book with an introduction by C. J. Friedrich was published at Cambridge, Mass., in 1932.

origin. Safeguard against external danger, wrote Mariana, one of the most prolific of the Jesuit writers, compelled families to unite and thus form a state. By their voluntary surrender the multitude choose a ruler for certain ends, chiefly the common defense. These ends are the measure of his power. Since rulers are chosen merely for convenience, safety, and the common good, they may not become arbitrary or oppress the subjects. A tyrant, Mariana argues, may be deposed. The right of tyrannicide against a lawful ruler who has become an oppressor may be exercised even by an individual.

In the *Tractatus de Legibus* of the Spanish Jesuit Suarez will be found the most complete treatment of law following the work of St. Thomas Aquinas. Suarez adopts the definitions of law laid down by St. Thomas and sees in each form some notion of justice as an ethical conception anterior to law in the narrower sense. In other words, to Suarez the law must be the embodiment of justice. Law was more than mere command because it implied right and justice which it did not create but which it recognized. The contributions of the Jesuits to politics and jurisprudence should not be overlooked. "They combined," as Dr. Figgis has said, "the new recognition of political facts with ancient ideals of unity, and the older conception of law, as an eternal verity."[13]

Perhaps the most important notion to emerge from the controversial literature at the turn of the seventeenth century was that of the social contract with the enshrinement in politics and jurisprudence of the conception of the rights of the individual. The contract of Althusius was far more valuable to subsequent political theorists than that of the Huguenots, who asserted that the compact was a bond between governor and governed, which settled the relations of each and was therefore above legal review. The rights of the individual asserted in the Renaissance and Reformation became legal rights. These rights when voluntarily given up and communalized became the rights of the state.

[13] A good account of the Jesuits will be found in J. N. Figgis, *From Gerson to Grotius* (Cambridge, 1907), Ch. 6.

At the same time that political theory was incorporating the social contract as a device for obtaining popular consent, the idea of natural law was preserved as a standard to which human laws must conform. Justice was implicit in the natural law, which is a body of principles devised by reason to make life secure. Men relinquish natural rights but only to insure the greater preservation of life, liberty, and property. They do not and cannot divest themselves of the natural law, which continues to be the measure of their competence in the establishment of legal and political institutions.[14]

THE SOCIAL CONTRACT PHILOSOPHERS AND JUSTICE

The social contract philosophers were heavily indebted to the Middle Ages, where the law was supreme because it was the expression of justice. These men agreed that justice can exist only in conformity to law, but differed in their conceptions of the source of law and hence in their interpretations of medieval theories of the law. To some the law was the will of the ruler. If the question were asked why the will of the ruler should be law, a ready answer could be found in the Digest of Justinian: *Quod principi placuit legis habet vigorem, utpate cum lege regia, quae de imperio ejus lata est, populus ei et in eum omne suum imperium et potestatem conferat.* In other words, the will of the emperor is law, but only because the people choose to have it so.

Elsewhere in medieval literature the idea was brought forward that the law was not merely an expression of the will of the ruler but of the life of the community. The law was embodied in customs which the ruler could not transcend. Legislative acts were not the expression of will, but records of promulgations of that which was already binding upon men. Among the Germanic tribesmen the spear clash gave law to the ruler and the ruled. Al-

---

[14] For an excellent but brief account of the theory of natural law, see A. P. D'Entreves, *Natural Law* (London, 1951).

though legislation as the source of law reappeared briefly in the empire of Charlemagne, it died out in the tenth and eleventh centuries and remained inactive for about three hundred years.

Throughout the feudal period law was considered to be custom, but laws had to be issued or promulgated by the prince or king. Without his authority this could not be done. In order to make his action legitimate, the king had to consult the great and wise men of his country. Bracton wrote: "The king is under God and the law."[15] In other words, the king must observe the will of God and the customs of the realm. But there is also in Bracton a further passage, which may have been interpolated, but which recites that if the king shall seek to rule without the law it shall be the duty of the counts and barons who comprise the great court to put upon him the bridle of the law. Undoubtedly the king in promulgating any law had to consult the leading men who surrounded him, but what he declared to have the force of law had to conform to the good usages and customs of the kingdom.

Whether the source of law was in the will of the ruler or the custom of the realm, it required promulgation by constituted authority. Men therefore turned to the examination of the foundations of political authority in their search for justice. From Roman law they concluded that there is in every independent society the power of making and unmaking laws, some final authority, which knows no legal limits. The reappearance at the end of the Middle Ages of this idea foreshadows the concept of sovereignty which Jean Bodin was to set forth at a later date in his *Six Livres de la Republique* and which Hobbes was to make the cornerstone of his theory of the state.[16] At the same time, other men clung to the notion that nothing has the form of law unless it emanates from the whole people and has their approbation. These divergent ideas

[15] A modern edition of Bracton's *De legibus et conseutudinibus Angliae* has been prepared by G. E. Woodbine and published by the Yale University Press in four volumes (New Haven, 1915–42).

[16] J. Bodin, *Six Livres de la Republique* appeared during the lifetime of the author in Latin and French editions. An English translation by William Knolles was published in 1606 at London.

of the source of law led to sharp differences among the social contract philosophers and gave rise to opposing theories of the meaning of justice.

Justice has always been a reality to those who were content to accept as just laws all rules emanating from competent authority. When Thomas Hobbes defined law as the command of the sovereign, he made it unnecessary for his followers to pursue the quest for justice further than the vindication of authority behind the law. Justice is the keeping of covenants. But the sovereign in any state can mean only those persons or groups of persons who dominate over the wills of their fellows. Justice then becomes identified with the will of that part of the state which is able to exercise political power.[17]

This realistic conception of justice does not satisfy the revolutionist who is discontented with the established law and order. Rousseau declared that justice could be found only in that state in which political authority rests upon the force of opinion which is truly public and general. In the attempt to organize such an opinion he introduced his idea of the general will, which he declared to be the only true sovereign of a state founded upon justice. Since by its nature the general will must be directed toward ends which are in the interest of all members of the state, it can never be wrong, and whatever it commands must be just. Justice, therefore, cannot be identified with the will of any part of the state, but must coincide with the interest of the whole body of the people.[18]

Neither the Hobbesian realist nor the idealist following in the footsteps of Rousseau has supplied a definition of justice that is adequate. Both theories when put into practice are reduced to the same terms. The general will of Rousseau requires interpretation, and into whatever hands the interpretation is placed will fall the exercise of political authority. In the end it may be that the bearers of political power are no more than a small part of the state.

[17] T. Hobbes, *Leviathan* (Everyman's Library).
[18] J. J. Rousseau, *Social Contract* (Everyman's Library).

THE FRAMERS OF THE UNITED STATES CONSTITUTION AND JUSTICE

The different conceptions of justice, as well as the sources from which these had been obtained, were fully understood by the framers of the Constitution of the United States. The men of 1787 firmly believed that the main objective of the state, whose fundamental law they were drafting, was the maintenance of justice. "Justice is the end of government. It is the end of civil society," wrote the authors of the *Federalist*. They then proceeded to show that injustice arises largely from the factious nature of man. That is to say, justice in the state is the resultant of justness in man. In order to attain justice, the spirit of faction must be curbed through the adjustment of conflicting interests in society. The realization of justice therefore involves the ceaseless task of subordinating the selfish interests of each part of the people to the permanent interests of the whole society.

The theory was that set forth by Montesquieu. James Madison, who had much to do with framing the Constitution, had studied carefully the pages of the observant Frenchman. Both men believed that if a government were so constituted that the vital political forces in the state were tied up in a nice poise and balance, the permanent interests of the people would be secured against innovation. To the inventive genius of Madison, government was a problem to be worked out by the superior minds in the convention without considering the opinions of the "unreflecting multitude."

Justice, according to Madison, ought to hold the balance among conflicting interests in the state. The Virginian was quick to see that the central problem of achieving justice is not the maintenance of equality, but the preservation of liberty. He argued that it was fallacious to suppose "that by reducing mankind to a perfect equality in their political rights, they would, at the same time, be perfectly equalized and assimilated in their possessions, their opinions, and their passions." As long as there was a diversity in the faculties of man, there would be no uniformity of interests. Madison regarded inequality as the natural condition of man, which the statesman must take into account in the formation of popular government.

The men of 1787 rejected the notion that a power altogether independent of the people be called to break and control the violence of faction. This task the people must themselves perform through the framework of their government. The people must be the makers of the law at the same time that they impose upon themselves the restraints necessary to the preservation of private rights. "In the extent and proper structure of the Union," they concluded, "we behold a republican remedy for the diseases most incident to republican government."

The framers of the Constitution of the United States were satisfied that they had secured justice within the framework of their document. The Constitution was "itself, in every rational sense, and to every useful purpose, a bill of rights." It was a "better recognition of popular rights than volumes of aphorisms which make the principal figure" in many earlier constitutions "and which would sound much better in a treatise on ethics than in a constitution of government." Justice, they said, "ever has been and ever will be pursued until it be obtained, or until liberty be lost in the pursuit."[19]

[19] For an account of the formative period of American political thought, see W. S. Carpenter, *Development of American Political Thought* (Princeton, 1930).

III

The Theory of Natural Law

THE LAW OF NATURE was exalted by the American colonists at the precise moment when the theory everywhere lay about them in ruins. Almost a quarter of a century before Thomas Jefferson in the Declaration of Independence appealed to nature and nature's God in behalf of the rights of colonial America, the theory of natural law had begun to crumble. David Hume had attacked both the theory of the social contract and that of natural law and argued that experience, and experience alone, could decide questions of morality and politics. His destructive criticism paved the way for Jeremy Bentham and his utilitarianism. To Bentham natural rights constituted nonsense, and imprescriptible natural rights nonsense on stilts. Nevertheless, the theory of natural law possessed great vitality drawn from the many centuries in which it had been nurtured.

From the time of Cicero to that of Rousseau, the idea of natural law cast a shadow over the minds of men as they pondered the problem of the government of men by their fellowmen. But it must not be supposed that the theory of natural law had an unbroken and continuous history throughout the centuries. The fact that Cicero and Locke used the term natural law does not imply that it had the same meaning for both men. To some writers the natural law was a body of higher law in subordination to which all human laws must be made, whereas to others it was merely a canon of interpretation for the positive law. Some thought of natural law as "a brooding omnipresence in the skies" whereas others sought to find in it an anchorage for the rights of man. Whatever may have been the meaning ascribed to the law of nature at any particular time and place, the concept was of great value in helping mankind to control his political destiny.

ROMAN DEFINITIONS OF NATURAL LAW

Practical application of natural law is commonly assumed to have originated with Cicero.[1] Although the Greeks spoke of the law of nature, it was unknown to the jurists of the Roman republic. Stoic philosophy conspired with Roman law just before the Christian era to declare with Cicero that "true law is right reason in agreement with nature." But in the minds of the lawyers of Cicero's time natural law was a reflection upon existing law rather than a philosophical principle controlling law. Institutions like slavery, which were contrary to the law of nature, were nevertheless justifiable and perfectly legal. As a pragmatic test of the validity of their own legal constructions, the natural law was of service to the Roman lawyers; it was not intended to stay their hands but to guide their minds. Because it had a functional purpose, the doctrine of natural law survived to become the *ius naturale* of the Roman jurists and a basic notion of the Christian Fathers.

The Roman jurists were not in agreement upon a definition of natural law. Gaius in the second century saw no distinction between *ius naturale* and *ius gentium*. A century later the more familiar trichotomy of Ulpian divided the law into *ius naturale*,

[1] R. W. and A. J. Carlyle, *History of Medieval Political Theory*, 6 vol. (London, 1903–36), Ch. I.

ius gentium, and *ius civile*. To this third century jurist *ius naturale* is little more than animal instinct. But Paulus, a contemporary of Ulpian, returned to a twofold division of the law into "what is always equitable and good, as is natural law" and "what in each city is profitable to all or to many, as is civil law." These divergencies were carried into the Corpus Juris of Justinian where the appropriate passages of the three jurists are recorded.[2]

Natural law to Cicero was to be apprehended by the reason of man as a result of his experience. Although there are no direct references in the writings of the lawyers to a primitive state of nature, their attitude on the institution of slavery would indicate that they believed man was born free but became enslaved according to human laws. Thus the distinction of Ulpian between *ius naturale* and *ius gentium* probably arose, and into the latter category were placed those institutions which distinguished mankind in society from a more primitive natural state. Hermogenianus, a late third century jurist, undertook an enumeration of the institutions of the *ius gentium*. His classification is ambiguous and by no means complete, but he gained for his work its inclusion in the Corpus Juris. By the time of Justinian the jurists, as a result of their own experience, were able to distinguish the *ius naturale*, the *ius gentium*, and the *ius civile* and to attach to each its peculiar characteristics.

THE CHURCH FATHERS AND NATURAL LAW

The Church Fathers, because they embraced a large number of men writing over a period of six hundred years, dealt with many topics. Their main interest was to promote the Christian religion. Perhaps the most important contribution of the Church Fathers to legal and political theory was their notion of property. The Roman lawyers had already advanced the idea of private property, but they thought of it only in a negative way. The maxim *sic utere tuo ut alienam non laedas* summed up about all that Roman law had

[2] *Ibid.*, Ch. VII.

to say about property. But if a man was to use his property only in such a way as not to injure another, he would not greatly benefit the Church.

Two distinct views of property appear in the writings of the churchmen. St. Cyprian in the third century took a view of property which is almost communistic. He was not supported by those who preferred the view of Lactantius that it is not property that must be abolished, but pride and insolence. If the rich would lay these aside, it would make no difference though one man were rich and another poor. The later Church Fathers were concerned to secure from the holders of property the funds with which to support church institutions. Almsgiving was taught as a Christian duty. In order to give alms, a man must have property in excess of that required for his subsistence. The Church therefore looked with favor upon property but insisted that it be rightly used.

As one might expect, the concept of natural law appealed strongly to all the Church Fathers. St. Paul in Rom. II: 12–14, set forth a law written in men's hearts and recognized by reason. Throughout the ages these sentences of St. Paul have been repeated in the belief that in them could be found a guiding principle for the control of human conduct. Centuries later, in the American colonies, Alexander Hamilton followed St. Paul when he wrote: "The sacred rights of mankind are not to be rummaged for among old parchments or musty records. They are written, as with a sunbeam, in the whole volume of human nature, by the hand of the divinity itself, and can never be erased or obscured by mortal power."[3] In other words, natural law according to St. Paul and Alexander Hamilton sprang from an innate moral sense and found expression in what we would call the conscience of the individual.

The idea of natural law in Cicero is somewhat different, as we have already seen. Cicero thought that men would recognize the law of nature through reason, but he expected that this recognition would come as a part of their experience rather than from an innate moral sense. In a number of the Church Fathers the Ciceronian

[3] *Works*, ed. Lodge, 12 vol. (New York, 1903), I, p. 113.

interpretation of the natural law is preferred. Cicero has had no lack of followers almost to our own day. James Wilson, one of the framers of the Constitution of the United States, expressed this conception of the law of nature when he wrote: "The moral sense comes to maturity by insensible degrees." If we will consult the history of mankind, "we may infer that the law of nature, though immutable in its principles, will be progressive in its operations and effects."[4] Whether the law of nature was to be discovered in human nature or in human experience, its existence was certified by all the Church Fathers.

The efforts of the churchmen were directed towards the identification of the law of nature with the law of God. Seneca had already depicted the state of nature as a state of innocence in which men lived in complete happiness. They passed out of this state through the growth of vice. Human greed destroyed the original happy state of man. It was but one step for the Church Fathers to identify the state of nature with the condition of man in the Garden of Eden before the fall of Adam. The principles which God intended to apply to mankind in the unfallen state were the principles which men must seek to find in the law of nature.

The aims and purposes of the churchmen become somewhat clearer when we look at their treatment of slavery. They accepted the notion that men are created free and equal. Slavery is the consequence of sin; before God the sinner is a slave. This does not necessarily imply that captivity of the body is required to bring about enslavement. A man may be a slave of fear or passion. The idea was thus established throughout the pages of sacerdotal literature that slavery is a remedial punishment for sin. In this way the Church Fathers were able to reconcile the existence of human slavery with the teachings of the law of nature.

The same difficulty confronted the Church Fathers in reconciling the rule of one man over his fellowmen that arose in the institution of slavery. Man is by nature made for society, but it is not by nature that man is the lord of man, nor is it by nature that man

4 *Works,* 2 vol. (Chicago, 1896), I, p. 137.

is in subjection to man. God made rational beings in His own image, not to be lords over each other, but to be lords of the irrational creatures. The government of man by man is not part of the natural order of the world. But St. Irenaeus in the second century traced the necessity of the dominion of man over man to the fact that men departed from God and hated their fellowmen. Rulership was therefore made necessary by sin and was a remedy for sin. Government is then a divinely instituted remedy for the sin and wickedness of men.

By emphasizing the sinful nature of man, the Church Fathers were able to reconcile both slavery and government with the natural law. They held fast to the notion that all men are equal in the sight of God, but they were equally vigorous in their assertion that God would punish sin. As long as sin existed in the world the subjection of man to his fellowmen would be just and right.

It will not have escaped attention that the Church Fathers wrote in a wholly different intellectual climate from the Roman jurists. The men whose writings gained for them immortality in the Corpus Juris sought to utilize the natural law to clarify and reinforce the positive law with which they were from day to day dealing. The churchmen were interested primarily in extending the Christian religion throughout the then known world. They saw in natural law a powerful solvent for doubts which might arise in the course of doctrinal disputations. Christian ethics, as well as law, could receive clarification by appeal to the principles of natural law. The functional character of natural law, which had made it so valuable to the jurists, was also helpful to the churchmen. In the course of time, the churchmen and the jurists joined to establish natural law as a cornerstone in the structure of law and order reared in the Middle Ages.

The final expression of the theory of natural law in the writings of the early Christians was given by St. Isidore of Seville, from whom it was copied into Canon law. The work of St. Isidore was in the form of a dictionary, or encyclopedia, and claimed no originality. "All laws," he said, "are either divine or human. Divine laws are based on nature, human laws on custom. The reason why these are at variance is that different nations adopt different laws." In this form the sentences of the seventh century Spanish archbishop passed into the *Decretum* of Gratian five hundred years later to form the foundation of Church law.

The incorporation of natural law in the *Corpus Juris Canonici* was a master stroke of political genius. Gratian was able to show that because of its divine character the natural law is binding and overrules all other laws. "Natural law," he said, "absolutely prevails in dignity over customs and constitutions. Whatever has been recognized by usage, or laid down in writing, if it contradicts natural law, must be considered null and void." But natural law was itself the product of human reason. It was an attempt on the part of man to recognize the divine will in human affairs. Man by availing himself of the natural law was participating in the wisdom of God. By its inclusion in a legal system, natural law became a link between the minds of men and the mind of God.

But the Christian church had for centuries lain under the admonition of St. Augustine: "What does it matter to man, in this brief mortal life, under whose rule he lives, provided the rules do not force him to do evil?" St. Augustine exhorted men to strive to attain the City of God, but this ideal was attainable, if at all, only through the grace of God. Human institutions should be directed wholly to the salvation of the soul. The corruption of human nature could be overcome, but not without the help of God whose wisdom was revealed in the Scriptures. It was therefore an important step in the development of natural law when it was identified with the word of God.

But Gratian's words, as D'Entrèves has pointed out, have a double meaning: "They mean that the law of nature is embodied in the Scriptures. But they also mean that the Scriptures do not contradict the law of nature. . . . Worldly and godly wisdom must be reconciled. Reason and faith are not incompatible."[5] If medieval Christianity was not only to bring salvation to the souls of men but

[5] A. P. D'Entrèves, *Natural Law* (London, 1951), p. 36.

also to insure their happiness in this world, faith could not stand apart from reason. The nature of man must be reconciled with the grace of God. This reconciliation was the great task to which St. Thomas Aquinas addressed himself.

ST. THOMAS AQUINAS AND NATURAL LAW

St. Thomas was helped to construct his philosophical system by the recovered Aristotelian learning. But most of his theory of natural law could have been built from the materials already at hand before he read William of Moerbecke's Latin translation of Aristotle's *Politics*. St. Thomas wrote "that the natural law is nothing else than a share of the rational creature in the eternal law." This conception the Stoics and the Church Fathers gave him. From Aristotle he obtained some concrete precepts for the application of natural law.

St. Thomas insists that there is in man a natural and initial inclination to do good which he has in common with all substances. The natural law therefore makes for the preservation of human life. Furthermore, man shares with other animals such instincts as sexual relationship and the rearing of offspring. Finally, man alone has a natural inclination to know the truth about God and to live in society. He will therefore be taught by the natural law to avoid ignorance and to do only those things which will not give offense to those with whom he must associate.

The natural law is not immutable and unchangeable, as St. Augustine appears to have believed. It is flexible and adaptable. It can change by additions where there is a natural inclination on the part of man to effect such change. Neither private property nor slavery were imposed by nature; they are the adoptions of human reason in the interest of human life. In these cases the natural law is not altered but added to. Likewise, the natural law can change by having something subtracted from it. If, for instance, something ceased to pertain to the natural law which was formerly part of it, the subtraction can be made without alteration of first principles. The natural law remains a general rule for the majority of cases to which it continues to apply.[6]

The system of natural law which found lodgment in the *Decretum* of Gratian, and which was developed by the greatest of medieval theologians, would not long have survived if it could not have received practical application. As we have already seen, the functional character of natural law appealed to the Church Fathers as well as the Roman jurists. They found it not only helpful in rejuvenating their minds but also in constructing rules for human conduct. But a political concept when it can no longer be related to political action tends rapidly to be discarded. This was not, however, to become the fate of natural law.

It is true that Machiavelli completely ignored the law of nature. But the Florentine was writing a handbook for political reform. He disclosed in the last chapter of *The Prince* his purpose to rescue his distressed Italy from the rule of petty tyrants. His method was to set up one great tyrant who would knock together the heads of all the little tyrants and establish order. Machiavelli desired efficiency regardless of the cost to the human spirit with which it might be purchased. There may, indeed, be times when the only way to secure the rule of law and order is to establish a military dictatorship. But Machiavelli's man of *virtu* must be forever content to live under dictatorship if this produces order and prosperity in the state. He may not measure the acts and rules of the dictator by a standard of higher law either of God or nature. The good man in the thought of Machiavelli is measured by his ability to attain power and fame.

THE THEORY OF NATURAL LAW BECOMES A DOCTRINE OF NATURAL RIGHTS

This aberration from accepted theories of law and politics did not stay the hands of those who were transforming the theory of

[6] Aquinas, *Selected Political Writings*, ed. D'Entrèves, (Oxford, 1948), pp. 123–7.

natural law into a doctrine of natural rights. The notion of natural law was accepted in the sixteenth century by Protestant as well as Catholic writers. Philipp Melancthon, the disciple of Luther, somewhat crudely sought to show that natural right includes all human relations consistent with the revealed commands of God or right reasoning about the nature of man. In other words, the practical rules of right living comprise natural right.[7] At the same time, Jesuit thinkers were bringing once more to life the notion that natural law proceeds from God and is anterior to the creation of civil society. Convinced of the sinful origin of the state, the Jesuits gave to civil power only a secular character. The state for them existed only for the worldly ends of peace, order, and material prosperity.[8] Unlike the Protestant sects, the followers of Ignatius Loyola rejected the idea that the state is to promote piety and religion. This is the function of the Church of which the Pope is the head. In the confusion created by the wars of religion and doctrinal controversies, the great work of Hugo Grotius appeared in 1625.

Grotius wrote in the midst of the Thirty Years' War which began in Germany in 1618. This was primarily a religious struggle and was waged with much bitterness and great destruction. Predatory armies scourged the country over which they marched, and all attempts to end hostilities through negotiation failed. Foreign intervention only complicated the situation and made worse the already desperate condition of the people. As accounts brought by travelers to Paris told of death and destruction throughout Germany, Grotius began his famous *De jure belli ac pacis*.[9]

"Fully convinced," wrote Grotius, "that there is a common law among nations, which is valid alike for war and in war, I have had many and weighty reasons for undertaking to write upon this subject." He further indicates that the wars then in progress influenced

[7] W. A. Dunning, *History of Political Theories: From Luther to Montesquieu* (New York, 1921), p. 16.

[8] J. N. Figgis, *From Gerson to Grotius* (Cambridge, 1923), Ch. VI.

[9] H. Grotius, *De jure belli ac pacis*, tr. by F. W. Kelsey. The Classics of International Law, No. 3 (Oxford, 1925).

him to write. "Throughout the Christian world," he said, "I observed a lack of restraint in relation to war, such as even barbarous races should be ashamed of; I observed that men rush to arms for slight causes, or no cause at all, and that when arms have once been taken up there is no longer any respect for law, divine or human; it is as if, in accordance with a general decree, frenzy had openly been let loose for the committing of all crimes."

The common law among nations to which Grotius referred is the natural law. The law of nature, which is a dictate of right reason, is to be distinguished from the law of nations. The latter is a law which is broader in scope than municipal law, and receives its obligatory force from the will of all nations, or of many nations. In order that he may construct his system of international law, Grotius insists that those elements which come from positive law shall be properly separated from those which arise from nature. "For the principles of the law of nature, since they are always the same, can easily be brought into a systematic form," he said, "but the elements of positive law, since they undergo change and are different in different places, are outside the domain of systematic treatment."

Grotius was clearly following the medieval thinkers in his definition of natural law as a body of rules discoverable by man through his own reason. But he firmly believed that the rules of natural law "would have a degree of validity even if we should concede that which cannot be conceded without the utmost wickedness, that there is no God, or that the affairs of men are of no concern to Him." In this respect he parted company with those thinkers of the Middle Ages who strove to identify the law of nature with the law of God. However, Grotius was not able wholly to secularize his conception of natural law. "The law of nature of which we have spoken," he wrote, "comprising alike that which relates to the social life of man and that which is so called in a larger sense, proceeding as it does from the essential traits implanted in man, can nevertheless rightly be attributed to God, because of His having willed that such traits exist in us." In other words, that which is contrary to the nature of man contravenes the natural law. There need be no theological foundations for a theory of natural law; its fundamental principles can be apprehended wholly by human reason.

It must not be forgotten that Grotius was writing a treatise designed to subject the conduct of war to the rules of law and to preserve uninterrupted the peace resulting from war. He did not discuss natural law further than was necessary to his purpose. He was interested to show the relation of this law to the purposes, methods, and results of war. In order to do this, Grotius was obliged to make some demonstrations. He observed that some things belong to men in common and are not susceptible of private ownership. Likewise, there are some acts which are "indispensable for the obtaining of the things without which life cannot be comfortably lived." The right to such acts as human life requires is a natural right. Thus Grotius uncovered the principle of natural rights.

The work of Grotius, revised and offered in several new editions, was at the height of its influence when the *Leviathan* of Thomas Hobbes appeared in 1651.[10] Hobbes did not have the same end in view as Grotius. The Englishman had fled to Paris at the outbreak of the Puritan Revolution and continued in exile about eleven years, when he made his submission to the Commonwealth and returned to London. What Hobbes aimed to do was to lay the foundations of a strong government which would rule through the steady discipline of fear. "Men have no pleasure," he said, "in keeping company, where there is no power able to over-awe them all." His Leviathan is a commonwealth endowed with all the necessary powers to achieve and maintain peace.

Hobbes from the outset displays his contempt for the philosophical system of Grotius. Where the Dutchman had painstakingly assembled the wisdom of the ages in support of the existence of natural law, Hobbes brushed this aside and boldly asserted that all

[10] There are many editions of Hobbes' *Leviathan*. I have used the one published in Everyman's Library.

law is the command of the sovereign. In other words, the head of the state alone can define and promulgate the law of nature.

By reducing all law to the command of the sovereign, Hobbes cleared away much of the confusion which had attended definitions of law since the Middle Ages. The laws of nature he recognized prior to the creation of a commonwealth not as properly laws, but qualities that dispose men to peace, and to obedience. It is only when a commonwealth has been established that the laws of nature can be made binding, and then solely because they become civil laws. "The laws of nature and the civil law," said Hobbes, "contain each other and are of equal extent."

Likewise, the divine law cannot be the revelations to private men in their dreams and fancies, but only that which is commanded by the commonwealth. It is in the laws of the commonwealth that one must seek the natural law and the law of God. The sovereign's formal judgment is required before Hobbes is willing to admit that any rule has the character of law.

In order to construct his system, Hobbes is obliged to oppose natural right to natural law. Most writers, following the thought of Grotius, have deduced natural rights from the law of nature. Hobbes defines natural right as the liberty each man has to use his own power for the preservation of his own nature, that is, of his own life. The law of nature, however, is a precept or general rule, found out by reason, by which a man is forbidden to do that which is destructive of his life. "Law and right," he says, "differ as much as obligation and liberty; which in one and the same matter are inconsistent."

The fundamental law of nature, according to Hobbes, directs man to seek peace. This can only be achieved through the surrender of natural rights into the hands of a sovereign who shall enforce the peace. The surrender is accomplished through the medium of the social contract, and is complete. The only rights which remain to the individual are not to be obliged to kill himself and not to be obliged to accuse himself. In other words, he retains only the right of self-preservation; all other rights become vested in the sovereign.

The teachings of Hobbes proved unpalatable to his contemporaries. No party in England found the *Leviathan* wholly to its liking, and on the continent of Europe the religious views expressed in the book were widely condemned. Machiavelli had ignored religion and morals for practical reasons; Hobbes placed religion and morality at the mercy of the head of the state. By declaring that divine and natural law existed only in the form of rules laid down by the sovereign, Hobbes assumed an extreme position that few men of his time were ready to follow.

An attempt to reconcile the conflicting views of Grotius and Hobbes on natural law was made by Samuel Pufendorf, a talented German philosopher, whose *De iure naturae et gentium* first appeared in 1672.[11] His state of nature is not like that of Hobbes, a state of war where men live in brutish reciprocal hostility, and the hand of each is against all. Men to Pufendorf are rational beings from their creation, and the dictates of right reason guide them, whether in a state of nature or under civil government. The law of nature teaches every man to "cultivate, and by his life promote, a sociable attitude so far as in him lies." Unfortunately, the majority of men do not follow the dictates of reason but give free rein to their instincts and impulses. The establishment of civil society therefore becomes necessary. "The real and principal reason," declares Pufendorf, "why the fathers of families left their natural liberty and undertook to establish states, was in order that they could surround themselves with defences against the evils which threaten man from his fellow man."

The internal structure of the state Pufendorf rests upon the social contract. But in his system there are two contracts, the first of which creates civil society and the second establishes the form of government. The first contract is the social compact introduced into political science by Althusius and Hobbes and entered into by

---

[11] S. Pufendorf, *De iure naturae et gentium*, tr. W. A. Oldfather. The Classics of International Law, No. 17 (Oxford, 1934).

those who consent to the formation of the state. The second instrument is the governmental contract made familiar by antimonarchical writers in earlier times, and which is formed by agreement between the designated bearers of governmental power on the one hand and the rest of the community on the other hand. By this pact the rulers bind themselves to the care of the common security and safety, and the rest to render them obedience. "When a democracy has been established," Pufendorf observes, "this last pact does not appear so clearly, since the same individuals are in different respects both rulers and subjects."

By the time of Locke, the individualistic spirit of the Reformation had permeated legal and political theory. The social contract was the accepted explanation for the origin of the state. In England the rebellion of Cromwell had resulted in extreme claims by the rank and file of the army in behalf of natural rights. A group known as the Levellers asserted that freedom of religion and freedom from impressment were not to be abridged by Parliament. In the *Agreement of the People*, this group concluded: "These things we declare to be our native rights, and we are therefor resolved to maintain them with our utmost possibility against all oppression whatsoever."[12]

Across the Atlantic in the New England colonies, the church covenants appeared to supply a foundation for authority in both church and state in the free consent of the people. Although the colonists acknowledged "the duty they owe their sovereign whose natural born subjects they were," they did not hesitate to model their local governments on their church organizations. To the Puritans of New England their church organizations represented on the one hand the logical culmination of the religious revolt begun by Luther and on the other the prototype of the only civil government consistent with their religious ideals. Independency carried on the reformation of ecclesiastical power in thoroughgoing fashion, until "the people of the particular churches should

[12] G. P. Gooch, *History of English Democratic Ideas in the 17th Century* (Cambridge, 1898), p. 151.

come in for a share, according to their places and proportions." The notion of contract therefore became equally valid to the colonists as the basis of ecclesiastical and civil government.[13]

To Locke, as he surveyed the thought of Englishmen at home and abroad, natural law was the necessary presupposition of natural right. His debt to Grotius and Pufendorf is apparent throughout his work. He admits the guidance of Richard Hooker, whose *Laws of Ecclesiastical Polity* in the days of Elizabeth restated the teachings of St. Thomas Aquinas to controvert the Puritans. But the thought of Locke was sharpened by the stirring events of the time in which he lived. To him the natural freedom of man is derived from his knowledge of the law of nature, just as the freedom of an Englishman—his liberty to dispose of his actions and possessions—depends upon his capacity to know the law of the land. Natural rights persist in civil society, according to Locke, and civil government exists only for the protection of those rights.[14]

The social contract in Locke, unlike that of Hobbes, is a limited agreement. Each individual agrees with every other to give up to the community the natural right of enforcing the law of reason, in order that life, liberty, and property may be preserved. Power is given to the community, and not to a sovereign as in the case of Hobbes. Indeed, the word sovereign does not appear in Locke's book. Furthermore, the contract is not general, but limited and specific. The natural right of enforcing the law of reason alone is given up; the natural rights reserved to the individual limit the just power of the community.

The great merit of Locke's political theory lies in his denial that sovereignty can exist anywhere except in the community as a whole. This is the original and supreme will which organizes the government and defines its just powers. Locke's conception of government is compatible with almost any variety of institutions,

[13] W. S. Carpenter, *Development of American Political Thought* (Princeton, 1930), Ch. I.
[14] Locke's *Two Treatises of Civil Government* will be found in Everyman's Library.

so long as it is recognized that the rulers are the trustees of the people who delegate their powers to them. Unlike the great French philosopher Rousseau whom he in part anticipated, and who denied that the supreme will could be represented any more than it could be alienated, Locke asserted that by the act of setting up a government the people divested themselves of the rights which they transferred to the government. That is to say, the function of governing became lodged exclusively in the government. It was enough for him that supreme power was vested in the people on the days of their elections.

The theory proved admirably suited to the practical politics of the eighteenth and nineteenth centuries. It came to America not only to provide the basic ideas put forward in justification of the Revolution but also to supply a formula by which written constitutions could be worked out. Natural law was absorbed as a feature of American public and private law, and natural rights reappeared as constitutional limitations upon legislative power. The formation or alteration of a constitution proved to be identical with an act of revolution. Nothing more was necessary to establish Locke's theory as a working hypothesis in the development of constitutional government.

MONTESQUIEU AND ROUSSEAU HAVE OTHER IDEAS

Meanwhile, on the continent of Europe the struggle for popular rights was kindled anew by appeal to other doctrines which boasted lineage as ancient as that of natural law. The work of Montesquieu, whose *Spirit of the Laws*[15] appeared in 1748, laid the foundation for the modern historical school of politics and jurisprudence. This enlightened Frenchman was less interested to explore the bases of legal and political institutions than to reform the existing political and social order. Locke had sought to justify the Revolution of

[15] The English translation of *L'Esprit des Lois* by Thomas Nugent has been reprinted in many editions.

1688 in England and, as he said, "to establish the throne of our great Restorer, our present King William, and make good his title in the consent of the people." Montesquieu sought to justify and at the same time to reform the French monarchy. He was convinced that France was unsuited to a republican form of government.

Montesquieu was chiefly interested to safeguard political liberty. This he believed could be achieved by constitutional construction. Indeed, he was certain that the British had already attained this objective through the separation and balance of powers in the government. Natural law had for him small appeal, because he conceived the laws to be "the necessary relations arising from the nature of things." In other words, there existed a body of principles which determined the nature of institutions and of legislation. All that was necessary, according to Montesquieu, was to discover the principles underlying the forms of government and to apply them to each particular set of conditions. The *Spirit of the Laws* seeks to make this discovery. Although the writings of Montesquieu were widely read on both sides of the Atlantic, they had nowhere the revolutionary impact upon eighteenth century thought which was derived from Rousseau.

Rousseau in his earlier writings depicted man in a state of nature as happy and carefree, a condition which he continued to find desirable in his later book on education.[16] But in the meantime he came to recognize that society and government, however deplorable, are necessary to man. In the *Contrat Social* Rousseau undertook to find some rational form through which their existence might be justified.[17] Dismissing force as the basis of the state, he concludes that political authority can have no rational basis except the agreement and consent of the people.

The social contract envisaged by Rousseau embraced the total

[16] Rousseau's ideas on education are to be found in the *Emile*. This book has been translated into English by Barbara Foxley and published in London and New York, 1911.

[17] The best edition of the *Social Contract* is that by H. J. Tozer, published in London, 1905.

alienation to the whole community of each associate with all his rights. The alienation being made without reserve, each member of the community can no longer claim individual rights, and all are equal. "In short," he said, "each giving himself to all, gives himself to nobody; and as there is not one associate over whom we do not acquire the same rights which we concede to him over ourselves, we gain the equivalent of all that we lose, and more power to preserve what we have." What the individual does is to relinquish his natural rights to the community to receive them back in the form of civil liberty.

The effect of the contract is to create a moral and collective body composed of the contracting parties but which has a life and will of its own. This general will constitutes a sovereign power which is indivisible and inalienable. Moreover, the general will is always right and always tends to the public advantage. The members of the community when they are deceived or blinded by self-interest may fail to recognize the general will.

From this standpoint we see immediately that it is no longer necessary to ask whose office it is to make laws, since they are acts of the general will; nor whether the prince is above the laws, since he is a member of the state; nor whether the law can be unjust, since no one can be unjust to himself; nor how we are free and yet subject to the laws, since the laws are only registers of our wills.

The acceptance of this theory involves a radical departure from all legal tradition. Human will is made the supreme arbiter of all human values. Moreover, for all practical purposes the will of the majority is to be taken as indicative of the general will. Human reason has been displaced by numbers as the source of all authority. When a triumphant majority has spoken, all that remains to the people is blind obedience. For Rousseau has said "that whoever refuses to obey the general will shall be constrained to do so by the whole body; which means nothing else than that he shall be forced to be free." In other words, there can be no standard of right and justice above and beyond the will of the majority.

There is a sense in which the will of the majority may be regarded as the foundation of human authority. Abraham Lincoln said:

A majority held in restraint by constitutional limitations, and always changing easily with deliberate changes of popular opinions and sentiments, is the only true sovereign of a free people. Whoever rejects it does, of necessity, fly to anarchy or to despotism. Unanimity is impossible; the rule of a minority, as a permanent arrangement, is wholly inadmissible; so that, rejecting the majority principle, anarchy or despotism in some form is all that is left.[18]

The principle of majority rule is therefore a device which, although it contains no inherent ethical validity, affords a practical means whereby groups of people may reach decisions. Whatever dangers lurk in the use of the principle must be curbed by constitutional construction.

But Rousseau did not regard his conception of the general will as a device; he thought he had developed a theory of sovereignty in which liberty and authority were reconciled. He was not wholly unaware of the lack of wisdom of the multitude, and said that the unenlightened would require the guidance of a legislator. But he never saw that human institutions must spring from the needs of the people and must be adapted to them as a result of slow growth. Reform to Rousseau meant the transformation of human nature so that every citizen is nothing, and can be nothing, except in combination with all the rest. When this leveling process had been completed, the sovereignty of the general will would be assured.

The ease with which Rousseau brushed aside the constraints of nature and of nature's God indicated the extent to which the theory of natural law had declined in the eighteenth century. The functional value of natural law to jurists and theologians culminated in the doctrine of natural rights. Natural law had withstood the assault of Hobbes and his insistence that law is the command of the sovereign. Men were unwilling to accept a theory which identified the theoretical sovereign with the person of the monarch. But Rousseau had established a sovereign in which the bearers of su-

18 *Works*, 2 vol. (New York, 1894), II, p. 5.

preme power are also the subjects over whom that power is exercised. The general will identified the makers of the law with those who were bound to its obedience. The sovereign of Rousseau possesses just as absolute and supreme a power as that of Hobbes, but it is a power not resting upon a contract of doubtful historical origin but upon the consent of the people freely given and constantly renewed whenever an act of legislation is required. "The sovereign being nothing more than the totality of individuals who compose it, neither has, nor can have, any interest contrary to theirs."

The natural rights of the individual become the natural rights of man. "There is never any need for the sovereign to give guarantees to the subjects," said Rousseau, "for it is impossible that the whole body should wish to do harm to all of its members." Safeguards against the infringement of individual rights are unnecessary in a state in which the owners of those rights are also the bearers of sovereign power.

Rousseau revived the community of Aristotle, but without the social element which was so important to the Greek. When Aristotle defined man as a social and political animal he meant that man's social characteristics engulf his individual desires. There is no place in Aristotle's scheme for the man who cannot live in association with his fellows. Rousseau, on the contrary, thinks of individuals as relinquishing rights to the community. There is thus fashioned a state out of the composite will of free and independent individuals. It is the lack of social consciousness in Rousseau that has enabled his conception of the general will to be perverted to base ends by some of his followers.[19]

It has been said that "the abandonment of natural law marks the rise of modern jurisprudence."[20] In the appearance of historical studies and the growth of positivism, jurisprudence assumed new forms which had not been possible while it was allied with natural law. The historical school, made possible by Savigny and brought

[19] See Leo Strauss, *Natural Right and History* (Chicago, 1953), Ch. VI.
[20] D'Entrèves, p. 96.

72

to England by Sir Henry Maine, undertook to account for the origin and development of law in a manner unknown to the metaphysics of the natural law philosophers. The destructive criticism of David Hume enabled Auguste Comte to lay the foundations of modern sociology. Although Comte was not immediately concerned with the law, his ideas enabled Gumplowicz and more recent scholars to develop the sociological school of jurisprudence.

Nevertheless, the theory of natural law supporting the rights of the individual has continued to influence legislation and judicial decisions on both sides of the Atlantic.[21] Many jurists have been unwilling to accept the separation of law and morals sought by the historians and the analytical school of jurisprudence. There has remained a tendency on the part of men to seek standards outside their governmental organs with which to measure justice and fair dealing. While the law of nature can no longer be conceived of as something static and eternal, "it is the stuff out of which human or positive law is to be woven, when other sources fail."[22] When an appeal is made to natural law, jurists are endeavoring to find that justice which lies behind the positive law.

[21] C. G. Haines, *The Revival of Natural Law Concepts* (Cambridge, Mass., 1930), Pts. IV, V.
[22] B. N. Cardozo, *The Nature of the Judicial Process* (New Haven, 1922), pp. 131–2.

IV

Roman Law and Procedure

ROMAN LAW HAS ITS recorded beginnings in the law of the XII Tables, the product of the decemviral legislation in 450–51 B.C. Its development ends with the codification known as the *Corpus Juris Civilis* ordered by Justinian in A.D. 528. In the intervening one thousand years the Roman legal system theoretically rested upon the XII Tables, which children at least in the time of Cicero were obliged to commit to memory in the schools.

The XII Tables is a code, which argues that it must have been preceded by a long period of legal development. The code embodied custom as well as some laws of the ancient kings, which the Decemviri had reduced to a single rule. It therefore denotes an advanced stage of the law, although the foundations on which it rests are unknown.[1]

[1] The best textbook on Roman law is R. Sohm, *Institutes of Roman Law*, 3rd ed. tr. J. C. Ledlie (Oxford, 1907). There are many worse books on the subject. The history of Roman law is splendidly done in J. Muirhead, *Introduction to the Private Law of Rome*, 3rd ed. rev. (London, 1916). The law of procedure in the Roman republic has been written by A. H. J. Greenidge, *Legal Procedure in Cicero's Time* (Oxford, 1901). A more recent study of Roman law during the empire is W. W. Buckland, *A Textbook of Roman Law from Augustus to Justinian* (Cambridge, 1921).

A code always requires interpretation, and to this the XII Tables was not an exception. Walter Bagehot has remarked that for a society to win in the struggle for existence two things are necessary, of which the first is that it shall acquire a legal fibre, a *ius strictum,* some set of rules, however elementary, that will give it cohesion and strength.[2] This requirement the Romans satisfied when the law of the XII Tables was put in writing, and so made more rigid the already customary law of the people. The other requirement, the same author says, is that when this law has become too rigid and too elementary for its possessor, owing to the increasing complexities of civilized life, some method of escape shall be found so that what was rigid may become elastic, what was primitive may be leveled up to meet more advanced wants. This means of escape the Romans at first found to some extent in the interpretation put upon the XII Tables by the pontiffs.

EARLY INTERPRETATION BY THE PONTIFFS

The practice of the pontifical college giving opinions on the law antedates the XII Tables. The pontiffs were the legal advisers of the ancient Roman kings and continued this service to the consul and later to the praetor. In general, the information was given only to the magistrates or to persons who were parties to an action and therefore practically concerned in some question of law. But about 254 B.C. the first plebeian pontifex maximus, Tiberius Coruncanius, announced that he would give information to anybody on legal questions. In other words, a knowledge of the law was to be made available to everybody and a system of public legal instruction was begun. This was necessarily accompanied by the beginnings of a juristic literature in which commentaries on the pontifical pronouncements appeared.

Thereafter the pontiffs found themselves sharing in the development of the law with juristic writers who were not of the priesthood. A technical knowledge of the law was becoming an ingre-

2 W. Bagehot, *Physics and Politics* (New York, 1948), pp. 53 *ff.*

dient of national culture. About 100 B.C. the great treatise of Quintus Mucius Scaevola, a pontifex maximus who subsequently became consul, appeared to set forth the *ius civile* for the first time in systematic order. Roman private law in the system of Scaevola supplied a foundation for all later legal writers of republican Rome. Although Quintus Mucius Scaevola asserted that no one could be a good pontifex maximus without a knowledge of the *ius civile*, his successors did not heed his warning. The later pontiffs abandoned the private law and confined their attention to the sacral law.

OFFICE OF PRAETOR CREATED

The office of praetor was created in 367 B.C., and the judicial functions of the consul were transferred to an official known as the urban praetor. His administration of the law was confined to the *ius civile*, based upon the XII Tables which had been cast in bronze and posted in the Roman forum. It was a law for Roman citizens only and was characterized by extreme formalism and rigidity. The praetor, officiating in his own court, was the supreme judicial authority. He was limited only by such popular enactments as the magistrates and the people had agreed upon and which had the force of *lex*. Such enactments were irrefragably binding upon the magistrates as well as the people.

In the course of time, many foreigners came to Rome to trade and some to reside. For these aliens the *ius civile*, because it was a law for Roman citizens only, afforded no protection and the court of the urban praetor was not for them a court of justice. As a result there arose a great many formless transactions the basis of which was none other than the good faith of the parties. In order to clothe with the protection of law these informal relationships in which one or more of the parties was not a Roman citizen, the office of foreign praetor was established in 242 B.C. To the court of the foreign praetor came a great variety of persons from Mediterranean countries bringing a diversity of causes arising from the growing trade and commerce centering at Rome. Since most of these causes required prompt settlement, the foreign praetor became skilled in the adaptation of the law to the particular cases before him.

The law which the foreign praetor administered was the *ius gentium*, or law for foreigners. The term does not appear in legal literature before the time of Gaius in the second century of the Christian era. *Ius gentium* is rather a term used by imperial lawyers to denote the treatment of law undertaken in the court of the foreign praetor in those cases where the *ius civile* was inadequate or inapplicable. For the most part the foreign praetor was guided by the *ius civile* which he stripped first of its formalism and then adapted to the settlement of the issues before him. In the course of this process, some profound changes in the law frequently occurred. While the *ius gentium* remained a part of Roman private law, it comprised a set of rules which were applicable to a greater variety of cases than the *ius civile*. At no time did the Romans import portions of foreign law into their own system. Whenever they borrowed from Greek or other systems of law particular institutions, they managed to give them a definite Roman character. But there developed an antithesis between the *ius gentium* and the *ius civile*, which Cicero remarked in one of his essays. The *ius gentium* received definite form for the first time in the edict of the foreign praetor.

The praetor did not have the authority to make law but he could grant or refuse an action. In granting an action he laid down the rules which would guide him in so doing. These rules comprised the praetorian edict. Both the urban praetor and the foreign praetor issued edicts at the beginning of the term of office which were designed to remain effective in each case for the year of their election. Indeed, a lex Cornelia of 67 B.C. forbade the praetor to depart from his edict, although he might issue extraordinary orders for such unforeseen occasions as might arise during his year of office. But the validity of the edict expired with the term of the praetor who issued it. The new praetor was not bound by the edict of his predecessor; he could alter it in any way he chose.

77

The office of praetor was only one in the *cursus honorum*, whereby a man moved from minor offices to praefect of a province or consul. The praetor was a politician who tried to conduct his office in such manner as would lead to his advancement. Roman politicians did not relish retirement to private life any more than do their modern counterparts. Hence a praetor tried to administer his office during the one year of his term in a way to give popular satisfaction. What each praetor did was to take those parts of the edict of his predecessor which had worked well and add to it constructions of his own which he hoped would prove acceptable. He discarded the unpopular or unworkable parts of the edict. Thus the edict became an instrument for the constant improvement of the law.

It was at the hands of the foreign praetor that Roman law in the period of the republic enjoyed its greatest development. The edict of the foreign praetor supplemented, assisted, and corrected the Roman civil law. In the course of time there grew up in the praetorian edict a kind of code of private law made up of the rules set forth by the praetor in the exercise of his judicial administration. This was a *ius honorarium*, or law made by officials. Strictly speaking it was not law at all, but the power involved in the right to allow or disallow actions. Nevertheless, Cicero speaks of the edict as a kind of law. Thus the *ius honorarium*, which consisted primarily of procedural remedies, developed into a legal system parallel to the *ius civile*. Although the *ius gentium* came to be applied in the court of the urban praetor, it was in the court of his colleague the foreign praetor where its influence predominated.

JUDICIAL ADMINISTRATION IN THE EMPIRE

The constitutional changes which took place at Rome in the first and second centuries of the Christian era had profound effects upon the administration of the private law. The power of the praetor to issue his edict belonged to peculiarly to republican magistracies; it was an exercise of judicial discretion flowing from the theory that the praetor had inherited from the consul all the judicial power which belonged to the ancient Roman kings. The rising imperial power could not long tolerate any rival independent authority. In the first century of the empire a number of statutory enactments curbed the power of the praetor in the conduct of his office. Finally, in A.D. 129 the Emperor Hadrian instructed the great jurist Salvius Julianus to revise the edicts of the urban praetor and the foreign praetor, together with some other official pronouncements, which, when completed, was ratified by a senatus consultum. This became known as the Edict of Hadrian.

The emperor became the source of all authority. It is true that this change in constitutional power did not immediately produce a revolution in the private law. The same magistrates continued to administer the law, but they derived their authority from the emperor and the procedural rules which they followed were not prescribed in the praetorian edict but in the Edict of Hadrian, which they were not permitted to alter. If any ambiguity arose in the rules of procedure, it was necessary to have this resolved by a rescript of the emperor. The free discretion of the praetor to supplement, assist, and correct the civil law had come to an end. Edictal law had become not praetorian but imperial law.

Meanwhile, the private law of Rome had already assumed the form in which it subsequently appeared in the Institutes of Gaius. The mystical influence of the number three which appears to permeate Roman legal literature led to classifications which are sometimes puzzling to modern students of the law. Tripartite divisions of the law characterize not only particular legal institutions but also appear in the classification of the whole of private law into the law of persons, things, and actions.[3]

THE LAW OF PERSONS

The law of persons deals with status. Modern law would regard it as dealing with abnormal persons. The purpose of this classifi-

[3] H. Goudy, *Trichotomy in Roman Law* (Oxford, 1910).

cation in juristic literature at Rome is to determine proprietary capacity. The status of a person is important in determining the extent to which he can have private rights. According to modern systems of law, every human being is as such capable of rights under the law. In other words, he is free, and as a result of his natural freedom the capacity of one man to have legal rights is as good as that of another. At Rome the situation was otherwise. There were persons who enjoyed no capacity for private rights because they were slaves. A slave, at least in the early law of the republic, was not a person but a thing.

There were other persons who, although freemen, were barred from the enjoyment of rights under the *ius civile* because they were not Roman citizens. Modern private law regards all men as equal before the law; aliens enjoy the same private rights as citizens. But aliens at Rome were permitted only those rights acknowledged by the *ius gentium*, unless stipulated otherwise in a treaty between Rome and the country of which the alien was a citizen. Despite the willingness of the foreign praetor to extend the protection of the law to aliens at Rome, the latter were subjected to many disabilities which did not apply to citizens.

Finally, the proprietary capacity of Roman citizens depended upon their status in the patriarchal family. Every Roman citizen was either a paterfamilias or a filiusfamilias, depending upon whether he was free from paternal power or not. Full proprietary capacity was vested only in the paterfamilias. The law of persons was therefore further subdivided into the threefold categories of freedom, citizenship, and family power.

Slavery was an institution of the *ius gentium*. According to natural law, all men were born free. Captivity in war made a man the slave of his captor, who might put him to death if he so desired. How much more humane is the captor who spares the life of his captive and makes him his slave! A man might also become a slave if he were condemned on a criminal charge. Of course, the children of a mother who was herself a slave were also slaves.

The chief concern of the early Roman law was to develop forms of manumission whereby slaves might become freedmen. Slaves who became freedmen were nevertheless subjected to political disabilities; they did not gain the benefits of full Roman citizenship. At the same time, the law undertook to protect the slave from brutal and inhuman treatment by the master. Especially during the empire, laws were passed giving the slaves some sort of legal protection.

Citizenship in the Roman republic and early empire was an important factor in the determination of private rights. Private law was a law that applied exclusively to the citizens of particular states; it was a civil law in the literal sense of the word. Roman citizens could therefore claim the full protection of the *ius civile*. Aliens, on the other hand, could enjoy only those rights which were acknowledged by the *ius gentium*. That is not to say that aliens were unable to obtain the full protection of some law. An Athenian could claim all the rights of a citizen of Athens under Athenian law. If he could not make a will under Roman law he could do so under the law of Athens. Conversely a Roman citizen could not make an Athenian will or claim the benefits of the law at Athens. The antithesis of mutually exclusive states is a fundamental principle of ancient life.

A situation of this kind was not conducive to the development of Rome as the world center of trade and commerce. For a time, special treaties between Rome and other Mediterranean communities afforded some foreigners opportunities to engage in trade and to contract marriages under the rules of Roman law. The final step was taken by Caracalla in A.D. 212 when he bestowed Roman citizenship upon all foreigners within the empire who were members of some political community. The only foreigners who were left were homeless aliens whose community had been destroyed and who could therefore claim no place where they were entitled to reside. From the time of Caraccalla, just as there was but one emperor and one empire, there was to be only one law. Roman law became the law of a vast empire in which almost everybody who was free was a Roman citizen.

The question of status within the patriarchal family is of importance only in private law. In public law the filiusfamilias is as much entitled to vote and hold public office as the paterfamilias. As a Roman citizen, the person under paternal power has, in general, the same private rights as the head of the household. The son can make contracts, acquire ownership in property, contract a valid marriage, and be instituted a testamentary heir. But whatever a filiusfamilias acquires, he does so for the paterfamilias. The exercise by a filiusfamilias of his private rights results in the accrual of all benefits to the paterfamilias. It is only the debts of a filiusfamilias that accrue, not to the head of his household, but to himself. In other words, a filiusfamilias has passive but not active proprietary capacity.

The law of family power has no modern counterpart because there is no *patria potestas* or patriarchal family. The idea that there exists in every household but one ownership, one marital and one paternal power, that of the paterfamilias, belongs to early Roman law. Already by the time of the empire inroads were being made upon the *patria potestas*, and the filiusfamilias was gaining active proprietary capacity. At first it was the soldier who obtained the right to hold in separate ownership any thing he acquired in war. Public officials were the next to obtain the same privilege. The emoluments of public office, the fees received from the legal profession, and gifts from the emperor belonged to the filiusfamilias and not to the head of the household. Finally, by the time of Justinian the filiusfamilias was able to acquire complete ownership in any thing he did not receive from his father.

THE LAW OF THINGS

The law of things is by far the largest and most important division of the Roman law as it appears in the Institutes of Gaius. It does not, however, fit into any modern classification. Roman jurists were only gradually attaining the clear-cut conception of a right which is basic to modern systems of law. In the Roman law the use of the term *thing* (*res*) is very broad. It ranges from the most general meaning of "everything that exists" to specific objects. Ulpian says: "The term *res* comprises both *causae* (legal relations, judicial matters) and *iura* (rights)." With reference to judicial trials, *res* means both the object of the controversy and the litigation itself.

What Gaius did was to explain the different kinds of property which were found at Rome, and then give an account of the means of acquiring and transferring the ownership of single items of tangible property.[4] This was followed by a discussion of rights in the property of another, such as servitudes, and the ways in which these were acquired, transferred, and lost.

The treatment of the law of things next embraces the subject of universal succession, which is defined as "nothing else than the succession to the whole right which the deceased had." This falls within the law of property, although it is in reality a law of inheritance. Universal succession involves the notion that the estate of the deceased is preserved in its entirety, with all its rights and liabilities, and passes as a whole to the heir or heirs. It goes back to a time when common ownership was in the family, and individual ownership was unknown. The individual dies but the family continues. The heir therefore succeeds to the personality of the deceased and assumes all his rights and liabilities.

Finally, the law of obligations is subjected to lucid explanation. It is this branch of the law which was most thoroughly worked out by the Roman jurists, because it had received careful attention at the hands of the praetor. Although the law of obligations is highly complex, embracing a great variety of transactions and relations, it forms one of the most logical developments to be found in legal literature.

Obligations arose, according to Roman law, from contract, delict, and analogous relations. "The substance of an obligation,"

[4] The work of Gaius has appeared in many editions. A recent edition of the text with critical notes and English translation is that of F. de Zulueta, *The Institutes of Gaius*, 2 vol. (Oxford, 1946–53).

wrote the jurists, "consists in binding another person to give us something, to do or to perform something." Obligations arose from wrongdoings, the wrongdoer being obligated to pay a penalty to the injured person, and from contracts when one party or both parties assumed obligations through agreement. Other kinds of obligations, which did not originate either in an agreement or as a result of wrongdoing, were embraced by a comprehensive term, *variae causarum figurae*.

The law of things therefore included incorporeal as well as corporeal things. Land, slaves, money, and other things which could be touched were, of course, *res corporales* in respect to which a law of property could be built. But the same branch of the law also included incorporeal things, which had no actual existence, which could not be touched, and which existed only in the eye of the law. These *res incorporales* comprise largely obligations. Their inclusion in the law of things makes this division of the law the most important, because it embraces all rights, whether relating to property or not.

THE LAW OF ACTIONS

The third major division of the Institutes of Gaius, the law of actions, deals with procedure. At the same time, one finds intermingled with forms of procedure a considerable amount of what must be called substantive law. It must be remembered that in the early Roman republic much of the legal procedure was in reality regulated self-help. Abundant evidence of this is to be found in the XII Tables. The chief aim of the procedural forms of the early republic was to get the parties into court where the issues could be joined and the dispute adjudicated.

The law of actions may be said to have passed through three stages in its development. The first stage is that represented by the legislation of the XII Tables. Judicial procedure under the decemviral system was by means of legis actiones. These, according to Gaius, were so called "either because they had been introduced by leges, legislative enactments (the edicts of the praetor, which were subsequently a fertile source of actions, not being then in use), or because the very words of the laws to which they were due were imported into them." Of the five legis actiones enumerated by Gaius only one, that *per condictionem*, was unknown in the decemviral period. The other four were regulated by the XII Tables and must have existed in some form anterior to them. Both in spirit and in technical form these legis actiones are substitutes for self-help. They represent a development from a more primitive body of customs in which private redress formed an essential feature. The essential characteristic of the legis actio was the use of prescribed oral formulae in the trial before the magistrate. Any changes in the prescribed words by one of the parties might result in his losing the case.

The second stage was reached in the formulary procedure instituted by the foreign praetor. As has already been said, it was the duty of the foreign praetor to adjudicate in disputes to which a foreigner was a party. In such cases the *ius civile*, intended for Roman citizens, did not apply and the legis actiones could not be utilized. The foreign praetor was therefore obliged not only to seek the rules to be laid down in his court in the *ius gentium* but also to develop a new form of procedure in which he formulated the issue in a written decree appointing the sworn jurors who were to decide the case. The formula was the written authorization given to a *iudex* (juror) directing him to condemn the defendant if certain factual or legal circumstances appeared proved, or to absolve him if this were not the case.

It was a fundamental characteristic of all procedure before the praetorian court that the proceedings be sharply divided into two parts. The first was the pleadings before the magistrate in which the issues were joined and a decision reached that the plaintiff had a case which was admissible at law. The second part involved the transfer of the action into the hands of a private individual, or several private individuals, who ascertained the facts of the case and gave judgment. Roman civil procedure required that the magistrate should abstain from deciding the legal issue himself, and should refer the decision to a private individual who was appointed *iudex* for the particular action. In this way the magisterial power was eliminated from the domain of private law.

The formulary procedure devised in the court of the foreign praetor was vastly superior to the legis actio system with its symbolic formalism. Within a short time the urban praetor, by virtue of his imperium, was allowing the use of the formulary procedure instead of the legis actio in suits between Roman citizens. The triumph of the formulary procedure was finally assured by the enactment of the lex Aebutia (about 130 B.C.) and the leges Juliae which abolished the legis actiones—except for the centumviral court and in the case of damnum infectum—and established the formula.

The third stage in the development of procedural law was reached in the empire. The downfall of the formulary procedure could have been predicted from the time of Hadrian, when the praetorian edict was deprived of its former effect. The formula had no real existence apart from the edict; when the latter became stereotyped through codification, the necessity to replace the formulary procedure with a system more congenial to the emperor became apparent.

Legal reform at Rome, as elsewhere, came slowly. The formulary procedure was gradually displaced by one in which the trial was conducted throughout by a state official. This was known as the extraordinary procedure (*cognitio extra ordinem*), which was based on the idea that the administration of justice is a function of the state, whereas in the previous forms of proceedings the trial was dominated by the parties under the supervision of the magistrate. Under the extraordinary procedure the private juror (*iudex*) disappeared and was replaced by a public official acting as the delegate of the emperor. The formulary procedure was abandoned in the provinces under Diocletian and was finally abolished at Rome in A.D. 342. Thereafter judicial administration was wholly in the hands of the emperor or his appointees.

RISE OF ROMAN JURISPRUDENCE

The interpretation of the law had before the end of the Roman republic passed from the hands of the pontiffs into those of lay jurists. This transition was hastened in the first century of the Christian era by the establishment at Rome of two rival law schools. These schools not only taught law but also stimulated the writing of commentaries. The founders of these law schools, who lived under Augustus, have long been forgotten, but their work lasted many years. The leadership of the more important school was assumed in the reign of Tiberius by a man named Masurias Sabinus, who appears to have written much and to have inspired his students to do more. The practice of writing commentaries *ad Sabinam*, that is, writing books on the subjects with which Sabinus dealt, established a pattern familiar in law literature. The most familiar copy in English law is Coke on Littleton. The original work by Littleton was a study of land tenures written by a fifteenth-century judge upon which Coke wrote his famous commentary.

The emperor adopted a practice of granting to privileged jurists what were known as *responsa prudentium*, or responses binding on the judges. That is to say, when a judge had brought before him a novel case, he submitted the pleadings to one of the privileged jurists and obtained from him a decision. From this decision he was not permitted to depart. Since the privileged jurists were scholars, they gave their decisions with some show of learning. Philosophy was added to legal knowledge to produce some general principles applicable to all similar cases. It is from the writings of these privileged jurists that many of the maxims and aphorisms of legal and political theory are derived. These men created the scientific jurisprudence of Rome.

The jurists reached the height of their renown in the third century A.D. Papinian, Ulpian, and Paulus lived in this century and were invested by the Emperor Caracalla with unusual authority. From the writings of these jurists the greater part of the Digest of

Justinian was compiled. When they had passed away there was little for their followers to do. These men became mere compilers as Roman jurisprudence began to decline. The right of the privileged jurists to give responses binding upon the judges ceased to be conferred after the close of the third century. By the time of Diocletian the Roman state was definitely established on a bureaucratic basis with an hierarchy of officials.

The ultimate decline of Roman jurisprudence is reflected in the "Law of Citations" of Valentinian III, promulgated in A.D. 426. Valentinian III merely sanctioned what had already become an established usage. He ordered that the writings of the most important jurists, citing them by name, together with the writings of all who were cited by them, should possess quasi-statutory force, so that their opinions should become binding on the judges. If the opinions differed on the same question, that opinion should prevail which was supported by most jurists. If the numbers were equal, Papinian's opinion should prevail, or, if Papinian had expressed no opinion on the question, the judge was to exercise his discretion.

THE ERA OF CODIFICATION

The time had arrived for the codification of the whole of Roman private law. Collections of imperial rescripts were published during the fourth century, which supplied a foundation for the Code of Justinian. An attempt was made by Theodosius to undertake the codification of the law which, if it had been carried into execution, would have rendered the later work of Justinian unnecessary. The Theodosian Code was in sixteen books and covered the whole field of law, private and public, civil and criminal, fiscal and municipal, military and ecclesiastical. The private law is in the first five books.

At about the same time, three comprehensive records of Roman law came into existence in the Germanic kingdoms which had overthrown the rule of Rome. These were the Lex Romana of the Ostrogoths, issued by Theodoric the Great; the Lex Romana

Burgundionum, issued by King Gundobad; and the Lex Romana Visigothorum, issued in Spain by King Alaric II. The purpose of these codifications was to provide Roman citizens within the respective kingdoms with legal rules for the protection of their private rights. These so-called Roman-Barbarian Codes proved defective, and were in time swept away by the great Corpus Juris Civilis of Justinian.

The Emperor Justinian in A.D. 528 directed his law minister Tribonian to consolidate the entire existing law in a single code. The materials were divided into jurist-made law, or excerpts from the writings of the jurists, and imperial constitutions, or statutory enactments, such as edicts, mandates, decrees, and rescripts of the emperors. To these was prefixed a short textbook descriptive of the whole of Roman law and designed for the instruction of law students. Thus the Corpus Juris Civilis consisted of three parts: the Institutes, the Digest, and the Code.[5]

The Institutes was based largely on the earlier work of Gaius, although it comprised four books. The law of property was separated from the law of obligations. The little treatise was completed and published in A.D. 533 at the same time with the Digest. Although intended as a textbook in the law schools, the Institutes had the same statutory force as the other parts of the Corpus Juris.

The Digest (Pandects), comprising excerpts from the writings of the jurists, was the most important task of the codification as well as the most difficult of accomplishment. Tribonian and his assistants had to survey an immense amount of legal literature covering a period of about six centuries of Roman law. They abstracted and arranged in fifty books the essential contributions of approximately thirty-nine jurists. The result is an impressive body of case law well arranged as to subject matter and readily accessible for practical use.

[5] There are numerous editions of the Corpus Juris Civilis. The most recent is that published in Berlin, in 1954 in two volumes by the photo-offset process. An English translation of the Digest begun by C. H. Monroe and continued by W. W. Buckland was published at Cambridge, 1904–9.

The Code (Codex) was a codification of imperial law. As in the Digest, the compilers were authorized to make appropriate changes in the constitutions of former emperors. Two attempts were required before a satisfactory compilation of imperial documents was evolved. When it was finally published in the middle of December, 534, the Code embraced constitutions from the time of Hadrian to the date of publication.

The collective title Corpus Juris Civilis appears never to have been used by Justinian, although the entire codification was issued to have statutory force, each part to have equal validity as parts of one and the same code of law. The writing of commentaries was forbidden, and all doubtful points were to be referred to the emperor himself for decision. Constant referrals to the emperor produced new constitutions which were subsequently collected and were known as Novels. The Novels constituted in reality a supplement to the Code but they came to be regarded as a fourth part of the Corpus Juris.

The heritage of Rome in the later Middle Ages was revealed to be twofold: Roman law and Roman administration. Of the two, administration was brought to England by William the Conqueror and his successors, but Roman law was left for the most part on the continent to become the foundation of nearly all European systems of law. Roman provincial and municipal administration proved to be of outstanding significance in the development of subsequent practices, but the Roman law was received in most continental countries as the main source of private law.

V

Germanic Law and Procedure

CONTINENTAL EUROPEAN LAW resulted from the fusion of Germanic customary law and Roman law. To these were added contributions from feudal law, canon law, and the law merchant. These latter bodies of law were administered by courts distinct from the ordinary local courts. Nevertheless, throughout the continent of Europe before the nineteenth century there did not exist any such thing as national civil law. In the earlier centuries there was an essential unity of legal development which transcended national boundaries. The idea that the different codes of modern states on the European continent have ancient roots in the special history of each country is largely illusory.[1]

Germanic customary law is one of the basic elements in the formation of continental European law. Before the Germanic peril to the Roman Empire became acute, the customary rules of the Teutonic tribes existed in unwritten form. Tacitus recites that in the popular assembly of the German tribe it was "permissible to

[1] Munroe Smith, *A General View of European Legal History* (New York, 1927), pp. 3–4, 40–1.

lay accusations and to bring capital charges."[2] Penalties were inflicted which were graduated according to the seriousness of the
offenses. The greatest penalties were reserved for those offenses
which tended to imperil or weaken the security of the tribe. But
the law of crimes and torts was sufficiently developed to permit
recognition of distinctions between injuries to individuals and
those which endangered the whole community. When codification
of the *leges barbarorum* was first undertaken, there had already
been many years of legal development in which the law had not
been set down in writing.[3]

THE BARBARIAN CODES

The Salic Law, if not the most ancient, is the most important of
the Germanic codes known as the *leges barbarorum*. Compiled
under Clovis towards the close of the fifth century, it marks an
important step in the great era of codification then in progress
throughout western Europe. Although the Corpus Juris Civilis
had not yet been compiled, the Codex Theodosianus, published by
the Emperor Theodosius II in 438, and promulgated in the same
year with statutory force for the Western Empire by Valentinian
III, had brought together the constitutions issued since the time of
Constantine and established a new body of Roman law. The work
had scarcely been completed when the Western Empire passed
into the hands of the German tribes, who proceeded to found their
kingdoms upon its ruins. In these kingdoms, however, there was
no attempt to subject the conquered Romans to the German tribal
laws, except in matters relating to the state. Within the domain of
private law the Romans continued to live under the system of law
to which they had been accustomed, while the German invaders
were governed by the tribal ideas and customs of their race. Doubt-

[2] *Germania*, tr. Peterson (London, 1914), p. 281.
[3] The most complete history of Germanic law is that by H. Brunner,
Deutsche Rechtsgeschichte, 2 vol. (2nd ed. rev. Munich-Leipzig, 1928). The
first edition was published in Leipzig, 1887–92. Nearly all subsequent writing
on the subject shows great indebtedness to Brunner.

less impressed by the clarity imparted to Roman law by scientific treatment, the Germanic kings embarked upon the compilation of the rules of private law contained in the customs of their people.

At the turn of the fifth and sixth centuries many compilations of the early Germanic laws were undertaken. The laws of Euric, the West Goth, antedate the Salic law. These ancient laws, which are substantially statements of old Gothic custom with some newer rules regarding the relations between the Goths and the Romans, were written in Latin with the probable assistance of provincial Roman lawyers. The laws of Euric were revised and enlarged by later rulers and became the basis of the Visigothic Code, designed to bind Goths and Romans alike. In the course of time, more and more Roman law, civil and canon, found its way into the code until it became distinctly ecclesiastical in its form and Roman rather than Gothic in its substance.

Langobard or Lombard law received its earliest statement in 643 in the Edict of Rothar. This is essentially a compilation of Lombard law and shows almost no ecclesiastical or Roman influence. There are no special rules regarding the Romans. Here as elsewhere, the Romans were subjected to Lombard law in all controversies between them and the Lombards, but were governed as among themselves by Roman law.

To this original code later supplements were added during the eighth century. The Lombards had then become Christians and the influence of the ecclesiastics became apparent. There was not, however, much Roman private law discernible in the code. Lombard kings in 746 and 755 made additions to the law through enactments in regular diets on the advice of royal officials and with the assent of the people. In the later Middle Ages Lombard legislation came to be recognized as comprising the best statutory law in Europe.[4]

[4] The treatment of early legal development on the continent will probably be most satisfactorily studied in the *General Survey of Continental Legal History* (Boston, 1912). This and the companion volumes published under the auspices of the Association of American Law Schools present in English much material that would otherwise be unavailable to American students.

Theoderic, king of the Ostrogoths, at the end of the fifth century extended his rule over large portions of central and western Europe. The Empire of the Ostrogoths for a time included the Danubian provinces, the greater part of Italy, the southern Alpine slopes, a portion of southwestern Germany, and southeastern Gaul. In the early years of the sixth century, Theoderic issued a code of laws described as an edict in which he stated that these were the rules Romans and barbarians were to observe. He made no attempt to establish a common law for Goths and Romans; in each case the rule binding the Goths was based on Gothic custom, and that binding Romans, on Roman laws. The edict of Theoderic lost its authority when the Ostrogothic rule was overthrown by the arms of Justinian and the law books of Justinian were introduced.

Among the Burgundians a compilation of customary law was made before the close of the fifth century by King Gundobad. For centuries this code remained in force and was applied in all disputes between Burgundians and Romans, but not in controversies between Romans. After the conquest of Burgundy by the Franks in 532 the code continued to exist as the personal law of all Burgundians, but did not apply to men of other German tribes or to Romans. Other codifications of Germanic tribal law, some of the records of which are scanty, were made during the period before the coronation of Charlemagne as emperor in 800.

The three comprehensive records of Roman law that came into existence at about this time have already been mentioned in the preceding chapter. Of these three records, the Breviary of Alaric, also known as the Lex Romana Visigothorium, was the only collection of *leges Romana* to gain widespread acceptance. It contested with the Corpus Juris Civilis of Justinian for first place as the compilation of law for western Europe. This rivalry ended in the twelfth century when the Bolognese glossators took the Corpus Juris of Justinian as the basis of their legal studies in the recovery of Roman law. From the beginning of the sixth century in western Europe there stood two types of codification, the one of *leges*

Romanae, or codes of Roman law prepared by the German invaders to govern disputes between the Roman subjects, and the other of *leges barbarorum,* or codes of customary law applicable to the settlement of controversies among the members of particular German tribes or to disputes between Germans and Romans.

The personality of law, to which reference has already been made, was no ancient Germanic principle. It was not recognized in the early codes, except between Romans and Germans. But by the time of Charlemagne the universal extension of the principle became nothing less than a necessity. Many different peoples had been politically united, but each continued to retain its peculiar traits and customs. The security of the empire would have been imperiled by an attempt to impose a single legal system upon diverse peoples not easily kept in subjection. In any event, it would have been inequitable, if not impossible, to permit special treatment of subject Romans without at the same time conceding equal status to the law of the various subject Germanic peoples. All the systems of law became of equal dignity.

Since everyone had his legal rights and duties determined according to his personal law, it became necessary that every person's law should be ascertainable. This could be done in a variety of ways, both formal and informal, but there was no liberty or choice. A man ordinarily had to choose the law of his native tribe or nation. Some exceptions to the rule of personality had to be made occasionally to avoid practical inconvenience, but these were few.

The laws of the Germanic peoples when codified did not cease to be customary law. Custom continued to comprise the bulk of the actual law of the invaders, and it was immemorial custom alone which gave any of these laws, whether written or unwritten, their binding force. The writing and formal promulgation were incidental, not essential to the character of law. In no case was the written law of any tribe a complete statement of the rules actually observed. The codes embraced only those matters which appeared to require formal statement. Fundamental rules of law were often omitted because they seemed so self-evident as not to need statement. At the same time, rules of an arbitrary character, such as the amounts to be paid as fines or damages for different offenses, were set down in detail. Thus the Germans brought to legal and political thinking a conception of law different from that of imperial Rome. "They habitually think of law primarily as the immemorial custom of the tribe, not as the legislative enactment of any supreme authority in the state."[5]

THE BEGINNING OF MEDIEVAL ROYAL LEGISLATION

Royal ordinances began to appear before the time of Charlemagne. These were given different names, but in the Carolingian period they were all called capitularies. Some of the capitularies were designed to supplement or to amend existing law. Some were to be incorporated in the law of a particular tribe, while others were made applicable to all the tribes of the empire. In principle these ordinances required the assent of the people of the tribe or tribes affected. There were other capitularies which represented an exercise of the king's public powers. The majority of these ordinances were administrative regulations dealing with the powers of public officials and with matters relating to the conduct of public business within the empire. Many, however, dealt with the maintenance of peace and order and practically created new law for all the subjects. Such ordinances overrode tribal law, although no approval of a popular assembly was required. To be sure, the assembly was sometimes consulted, because no fixed line then divided the royal and popular prerogatives.

The capitularies were not without effect upon the entire law of the Carolingian empire. While they did not supplant the existing systems of Germanic law, but stood alongside of them, the royal ordinances served to give unity of purpose to law in general. Royal law was territorial, whereas tribal law was personal. Although the

[5] C. H. McIlwain, *Growth of Political Thought in the West* (New York, 1932), p. 170.

Frankish rulers were unable to establish themselves as Bishop Agobard proposed, so that the realm might be ruled by one law as by one king, considerable progress was made toward minimizing divergencies and unifying the law. Royal law, whether developed through ordinances or through the decisions of royal courts, was in this period the chief method of legal reform. Royal innovations were introduced into tribal law, and thus continued as local custom after the successors of Charlemagne had lost their empire. In the family quarrels which brought about the dissolution of the empire, central authority disappeared and with it the royal ordinances which depended for their authority on royal administration. The capitularies either became parts of Germanic tribal law or disappeared entirely.

THE SALIC LAW

The Salic law is not a political law; it is in no way concerned with the succession to the throne of the kingdom. It consists mainly of a tariff of penalties, which shows the amount of fines for various offenses, and a short sketch of the procedure to be followed in obtaining judgments. Other branches of law, dealt with by custom, are dismissed in seven titles. Among the few civil law enactments is the famous chapter on succession to private property (Title LIX), which declares that no woman shall inherit land. Otherwise the position of women before the law was favorable. They were safeguarded from insult by heavy fines and their killing was subjected to the most extreme penalties found in the code.[6]

The procedure of the Salic law is not a system of proof but a process of coercion. The object is not to test the truth or falsity of a claim but to compel someone to give satisfaction. This is true not

[6] The text of the Salic Law is contained in Hessels and Kern, *Lex Salica* (London, 1880). An English translation of portions of the law will be found in E. F. Henderson, *Select Historical Documents of the Middle Ages* (London, 1912), pp. 176–89. The procedure of the Salic law is described in R. Sohm, *Der Procesz der Lex Salica* (Weimar, 1867). See also H. Geffcken, *Lex Salica* (Leipzig, 1898).

only of the executive procedure, which was available in certain cases for the recovery of debts, but also of the judicial procedure, which was reserved for cases of private wrongs. The executive procedure was set in motion by the individual and was not under the control of the court. Its object was to obtain from the presiding officer of the hundred court a ruling which would permit a creditor to undertake the extrajudicial seizure of the property of his debtor. It was also used to obtain the assistance of the court to drive from the land a person who had settled there without the consent of the inhabitants. The procedure required that the defendant be summoned into court, but it assumed that he would refuse to appear. The absence of the defendant was no bar to the regular course of the proceedings. In effect, the executive procedure was an exercise of the right of revenge regulated by a few simple rules of law.

The judicial procedure of the Salic law was designed to lead to a judgment in the hundred court. Since it was available only in cases of private wrongs, the defendant was obliged to make a response satisfactory from the point of view of the procedure. The summons, which was given by the plaintiff in the presence of witnesses, directed the defendant to appear in court after a reasonable period of delay. If he did not appear, the court had no power to pronounce and execute a judgment against him. The law imposed a fine of fifteen solidi upon a contumacious defendant, but this did not give the plaintiff his legitimate satisfaction. It is therefore probable that the court gave judgment against the absent defendant solely for the purpose of advancing the proceedings. For the plaintiff was now obliged to cite his opponent before the king. It was no longer possible for a contumacious defendant to escape the extreme penalty of the law; the ban of outlawry pronounced by the king concluded the proceedings. Thus the judicial procedure of the Salic law terminated either in execution, whereby the plaintiff secured satisfaction, or by the banishment of a contumacious defendant.

Judicial administration under the Salic law was carried out in popular courts, called hundred courts. To the courts came all the freemen as judges, and decisions were reached in the manner of a town meeting by popular vote. The methods of proof were by wager of law or by ordeal. There was no public prosecutor and nothing corresponding to indictment. The initiation of proceedings was wholly in the hands of the injured party, and the whole aim of the procedure was to induce men to submit to a decision of the court instead of helping themselves to the property of a debtor or prosecuting the feud against those who had injured him. The provisions of the law were not less advantageous to the plaintiff than to the defendant, since the obligation to prosecute a feud might become so burdensome that it caused one to withdraw from his kin.

The extent to which the king exercised control over the hundred courts of the Salian Franks appears at first glance to be slight. When the decisions of the freemen met with disobedience the only penalty was outlawry. That is to say, the man who would not abide by the decision of the court went out of the law. No administrative machinery was available to enforce the decrees of the court. But, as Sir Henry Maine has pointed out, it is precisely at this point that royal authority came to the aid of civil justice. The unsuccessful litigant who had agreed to abide by the decision of the court would find himself forced to obedience by the king's officer; and even in the absence of such an agreement, if the litigant who had been successful petitioned the king in person, the king would do him justice.

The *bannum* of the Frankish kings was not less important than the *ius edicendi* of the Roman magistrates, and actually had the same effect. Neither could be said to make law but both promulgated law in form designed to secure its obedience. The ban of the king was not a penalty for wrongdoing to a private individual, but punishment for an offense against the king in violating his royal command. Thus the royal power of commanding the observance of the law became no less important than the law itself.[7]

[7] The classroom lectures of Professor Munroe Smith have been published under the title *Development of European Law* (New York, 1928). This book contains a great deal of material on the formative period of European legal institutions not readily available elsewhere in English.

THE IMPACT OF FEUDALISM

Before the dissolution of the empire built by Charlemagne, the feudal system had been established. No attempt is made here to describe or to analyze the institutions of feudalism. This has already been done in comprehensive studies.[8] But mention must be made of the impact of feudalism upon the law of continental Europe. Feudalism is a transitional stage in the development of European civilization. On the one hand, it marked the abandonment of the principal of personality for that of territoriality of the law. The place where one lived and not the race to which he belonged determined the law for him. On the other hand, feudalism as a system of land tenures strengthened the political authority not only of the king but also of each feudal superior over those who owed him duties and obligations. The system was one in which all the land of the realm was drawn into the service of the realm, and those who rendered service to the community received, in the form of yield or produce of land, compensation for their services. The system required a high degree of complex administration which was greatly decentralized at the same time that it prescribed among the feudatories definite legal relationships.

Many causes conspired to solidify the law territorially. Perhaps the most important of these was the mingling of races regionally as the nomadic tribes settled on the land. As the feudal system developed, differences of race within each fief disappeared. All were but vassals within the fief, with the same rights and duties to their lord. Beneath the entire network of fiefs lay a common feudal law. Although the law still remained immemorial custom, handed down by one's ancestors, it became the custom of the district. The substitution of a single rule for a multiplicity of rules gained steadily throughout the feudal period. Although there existed for the continent of Europe no central judicial or legislative authority,

[8] The older accounts by Waitz, Seignobos, and Stubbs are still excellent. See also H. Mittieis, *Lehnrecht und Staatsgewalt* (Weimar, 1933), and M. Bloc, *La Société Féodale*, 2 vol. (Paris, 1939–40). A book of sound scholarship but more popular in form in English is C. Stephenson, *Medieval Feudalism* (Ithaca 1942). See also F. L. Ganshof, *Feudalism* (London, 1952).

feudal law was nevertheless substantially uniform. This was due chiefly to the similarity of conditions in most parts of Europe. The uniformity of the rules of feudal law made possible at the close of the eleventh or beginning of the twelfth century a private compilation known as the *Libri feudorum*. Other compilations of feudal law were made in the twelfth and thirteenth centuries, the most important of which were the *Sachsenspiegel* and the *Schwabenspiegel*. These collected customs defined territorially the immemorial custom of the community.

At the same time that territorial law replaced personal law based upon race, disintegrating tendencies appeared in the administration of justice. The king or other territorial prince continued in theory to be the head of the realm just as he was feudal overlord in whose name all lands and offices were held. But the king could demand political services only from his immediate vassals and these in turn could only require services from those who were subinfeudated to them.

The mutual obligations created by fealty and homage were of a personal character, and so could affect nobody outside the two contracting parties. No legal relationship was established between the lord and the sub-vassal. This rule was formulated in France in the fourteenth century—"the vassal of my vassal is not my vassal"—but was certainly then no novelty.[9]

The effect of this rule or practice was to place in the hands of territorial rulers, such as princes, dukes, and counts, great powers which made them largely independent of the crown. The situation on the continent of Europe was in strong contrast with that of England, where William the Conqueror required all landowners to take the oath of fidelity to himself, regardless of whose men they were.

Nevertheless, feudal relationships on the continent did not consist of abstract principles; they were legally enforceable. Failure on the part of either lord or vassal to observe the obligations binding upon him led to litigation in the feudal court. Although the lord presided over the feudal court, the court in principle was com-

[9] Ganshof, p. 88.

posed of all the vassals, and the judgment of the court was the judgment of its members. From the feudal court in England an appeal lay to the county court and, with the consent of the king, to the "great court." But in continental countries the administration of justice, except in feudal matters, remained in the hands of local courts administering local customs. Local customs had become territorial law, but the kings and even the great territorial princes lacked the power to draw into their courts cases where justice had been denied. The result was that feudal law stood alongside the territorial law enforced in the popular courts of the community. This dichotomy appeared in the thirteenth century compilations. The *Sachsenspiegel* includes a law-book of territorial and one of feudal law. The same is true of the *Spiegel der deutschen Leute*, which appeared in South Germany about 1250. It is based on the *Sachsenspiegel*, but undertakes to present a common law for Germany. The book was soon displaced by the *Kaiserliches Land-und Lehnrecht*, sometimes called the *Schwabenspiegel*, in which an attempt was made to present all Germanic law.

Meanwhile, the Church was developing a body of law and an ecclesiatical jurisdiction which embraced the whole of Christendom. Church law, which began before the fall of the Roman Empire, was derived from the Bible, the decrees of Church councils, letters of the Bishops of Rome on public and judicial matters, and the writings of the Church Fathers. From these sources there arose various collections of canons which were largely formless. It was not until the twelfth century that Gratian, a churchman who had probably been trained in the law school at Bologna, undertook the codification of Church law in his *Decretum*. This famous work, modeled after the recovered Roman law, laid the foundations for the Corpus Juris Canonici.[10]

---

[10] The literature on canon law is abundant, but much of it is not helpful to students of law and politics. A survey of sources will be found in A. Tardif, *Sources du Droit Canonique* (Paris, 1887). Students will be greatly helped by reading E. Troeltsch, *The Social Teaching of the Christian Churches*. Tr. O. Wyon. 2 vol. (New York, 1931). The first volume especially deals with medieval Christianity.

Among the Teutonic peoples each king was head of the Church in his own kingdom. In the Visigothic Empire the leading churchmen obtained a controlling influence not only in ecclesiastical but also in secular affairs. But among the Franks the Church was subject to the supreme authority of the king and was largely independent of Rome. Without royal approval, the Pope could not interfere with the Frankish Church. In the time of Charlemagne relations between the Pope and the king became closer, but the king continued to legislate in matters of ecclesiastical polity without necessarily consulting Church parliaments or synods. Bishops and abbots were regarded as royal officials and as such attended the parliaments and advised on legislation. This gave them an influence in secular matters.

Ecclesiatical courts arose during the Roman Empire when bishops settled many controversies among Christians. But the separate and exclusive jurisdiction exercised by the ecclesiastical courts developed slowly through the Middle Ages. In the empire of Charlemagne the clergy were in principle subject to the jurisdiction of the ordinary courts. In matters of faith and morals the Church not only enjoyed complete jurisdiction over clergy and laity, but also received the support of the civil authority. A person who was excommunicated, and who refused to make submission to the Church and do penance, might be banished. Behind excommunication lay the penalty of civil outlawry.

The collapse of the Carolingian empire left the Church as the only institution which appeared to stand for the unity of the Christian world. It is not surprising, therefore, to find the extension and consolidation of ecclesiastical power as the temporal power became more and more decentralized. Church courts began to claim jurisdiction over clergymen and to press for the right to adjudicate cases involving laymen where the offenses charged constituted sin. In many of these cases the Church had only concurrent jurisdiction with that of the ordinary courts, but in their control over marriages the ecclesiastical courts came to enjoy almost undisputed jurisdiction. The jurisdiction of the Church over marriages was extended to a great many matters of family law. Questions involving the legitimacy of children, the probate of wills, and the distribution of intestate property were readily brought before ecclesiastical tribunals.

An excellent system of courts was established to administer justice under Church law. Ordinarily the court of first instance was that of the bishop, who delegated his judicial powers to a subordinate cleric. But there were also lower courts which exercised petty jurisdiction and reached into the lives of the common people to a degree not attained by any other tribunals. From all of these courts, including that of the bishop, an appeal could be taken to Rome. The papal court at Rome also had original jurisdiction in all matters cognizable before the lower ecclesiastical courts. Since cases seldom came to Rome unless there was some doubt as to the law to be applied, the judicial system of the Church was a powerful agency in securing uniformity in the law and certainty in its application.

The theories of law which inspired the churchmen were largely derived from the Roman law as interpreted by St. Isidore of Seville. The definitions contained in the encyclopedia of the Spanish archbishop formed the core of the compilation of Gratian. The identification of natural law with divine, and of human law with custom, is basic to all ecclesiastical reasoning on the nature of law. Gratian did little more than restate in orderly fashion the ideas which had long been current among churchmen and which had controlled the decisions of ecclesiastical courts.

The canon law must be distinguished from the unchangeable law of God, which neither Pope nor temporal ruler could alter or disregard. But the canons of the Church embraced all the immutable divine law and thereby became instruments through which to disseminate a knowledge of the will of God among men. The canon law was therefore enabled to influence the legal development of western Europe to a degree not achieved by many other forms of law.

The medieval cities also played an important part in the development of European law. The cities from the North Sea to the Mediterranean littoral were centers of trade and commerce. In northern Europe the fairs and markets afforded merchants regular opportunities to display their wares. In the course of their mercantile transactions these men developed a large body of customs which came to have the form of law. These customary rules became known as the law merchant.[11]

The beginnings of the law merchant antedate the rise of Greek civilization. Commercial law continued through the ages to be unwritten and customary. Although commercial and maritime law was subjected to codification, it still remained the customs of the merchants which were changed as new conditions required. In the Italian cities the merchants gained control of the government and laid the foundations for the law of municipal corporations. Elsewhere the law of the market tended to become the law of the city.

The merchants required an administration of the law which was both certain and speedy. Time was short at the fairs and at the trading points in the maritime cities. Disputes arising out of mercantile transactions had to be settled while the parties were on the ground. The courts to which the merchants took their cases became known as "piepowder" courts and were invested with their jurisdiction not because of the parties appearing before them but because of the commercial transactions which they adjudicated. In modern times the law merchant has been codified in the law of negotiable instruments.

European law in the Middle Ages comprised the customary law of the Germanic peoples. Before the thirteenth century very little of this law was set down in writing. Each community had its local customs, which, having the force of law, were obeyed within the

[11] The law merchant is discussed in the general histories of English law, such as Holdsworth, and Pollock and Maitland. An excellent account of the early history of the law merchant will be found in W. Mitchell, *Essay on the Early History of the Law Merchant* (Cambridge, 1904). See also F. R. Sanborn, *Origin of Early English Maritime Law* (New York, 1930). The classic work on the history of commercial law is L. Goldschmidt, *Handbuch des Handelsrechts* (3rd ed. Stuttgart, 1891).

jurisdiction. Across the mosaic of local laws fell the shadows of feudal law, church law, and the law merchant, and at a later date the recovered Roman law. But most of this law had subsidary force only; it could be claimed only where no rule of customary law could be found to apply. With the exception of England, there was nowhere in Europe a common law for all the people of the realm.

Attempts to fuse the disparate elements in European law began with the Visigothic code. This compilation, which was largely of ecclesiastical manufacture, was greatly influenced by the earlier Roman law. The Frankish kingdom saw the beginnings of a common law of the realm. If the empire set up by Charlemagne had survived, it is possible that the greater part of Europe would have been governed, as England came to be, by uniform law. But the disintegration of political authority after the death of Charlemagne left on the continent no royal power capable of reconciling the conflicts among legal rules derived from different origins.

The growth of a common law for the continent was further retarded by the lack of experts trained in the law. Some statutory law existed, but most legal questions had to be settled by the unwritten and unenacted customary law, which had to be "found" or ascertained for the purpose. Law-finding was the task of the lay-judges or *schöffen* in the folkmoots, who gave their judgments without expert guidance. What these men knew of law was gained from a very narrow range of personal experience or suggested by practical wisdom. However shrewd the *schöffen* might be, they were unable to introduce into their judgments scientific precision or to view the law apart from popular conceptions. German law was therefore crippled by particularistic tendencies and by a lack of professional learning.

The European continent in the later Middle Ages required two things to adapt the law to the social and economic needs of the time. The first was a system of courts administered by learned judges to replace the communal courts presided over by lay judges. The second was the establishment of centers for the study and development of the law. The two are intimately connected, for learned judges can arise only where legal studies are being prosecuted intelligently and systematically.[12]

The scientific and systematic study of the law began in the twelfth century with the law schools at Bologna and elsewhere in Italy and southern France. But it was Roman law and not German law to which the learned doctors of these schools addressed themselves. By taking up the Corpus Juris of Justinian the Bolognese glossators not only recovered the Roman law but also put it in form where it could triumph over the folklore of the German communal courts. In the competition between the Roman law and the Germanic customary law, the learned world was on the side of Roman law.

But Roman law could have existed only as subsidiary law if the courts had not come to be staffed by judges trained in the Corpus Juris as interpreted by the glossators. Only in some jurisdictions in northern Germany did preference continue to be expressed for the *Sachsenspiegel*. Elsewhere, the customary law was almost overwhelmed by the contempt heaped upon it by the learned doctors who appeared in the courts. The final step which was to establish Roman law as the common law of the empire was taken in 1495, when the Reichskammergericht was created as a central imperial court. This tribunal ruled that doctrines not recognized by the glossators were not to be taken into account by the judges, unless proved. By this ruling what is called the "reception of Roman law" was accomplished.

[12] P. Vinogradoff, *Roman Law in Medieval Europe* (London, 1909). The competition between Roman and Germanic law is discussed in all general histories of European law. Munroe Smith's *Development of European Law*, pp. 227–292, is a brief but excellent account in English.

VI

The Laws and Customs
of the English

ENGLISH LAW BY THE thirteenth century, when Bracton wrote his famous treatise, had attained form and substance. A centralized judicial system had been created. England was well advanced towards the possession of a common law, which was being written not only in the assizes of the king but also in the decisions of the judges.[1] This was not true in earlier centuries.

LAW BEFORE THE NORMAN CONQUEST

The origins of English law must be sought in the customs of the Germanic tribes which invaded Britain and made the island their

[1] The most comprehensive history of English law is W. S. Holdsworth, *A History of English Law*, 13 vol., 3rd ed. (London, 1922–52). The best account of English law to the reign of Edward I is Pollock and Maitland, *History of English Law*, 2 vol. 2nd ed. (Cambridge, 1952). An excellent treatise in one volume is E. Jenks, *A Short History of English Law* (Boston, 1913). This is somewhat technical for beginning students. An excellent but very general treatment of English law will be found in Maitland and Montague, *A Sketch of English Legal History*, ed. Colby (New York, 1915).

homeland. Some codes of Anglo-Saxon law were written as early as 600, but these were compilations of existing customs. Even the code of the great King Alfred had little by way of innovation. "I durst not venture to set down in writing much of my own," said Alfred, "for it was unknown to me what of it would please those who should come after us."[2] He was therefore very cautious about the additions which he made to the laws of his ancestors and equally cautious about rejecting earlier laws and customs.

Codification became an accepted method of dealing with both Roman and Germanic law beginning in the sixth century. The Corpus Juris of Justinian was matched by codes of *leges barbarorum* such as the Lex Salica. The Germanic codes were crude and fragmentary compared with the great compilation of Justinian. But the Anglo-Saxon rules were even less comprehensive than the codes struck off among the Germanic tribes on the continent. They were set down in the language of the people, whereas continental codifiers, availing themselves of men of learning, wrote in Latin. Indeed, the Anglo-Saxon compilations hardly deserve to be called codes. They are little more than tariffs of fines and compositions to be paid where injuries have been inflicted. The great bulk of the law remained in the customs of the people which received no complete exposition, except in the judgments rendered by the popular courts.[3]

Judicial administration among the Angles and Saxons was fully developed in the hundred court before the migration of these tribes from the continent. The smaller unit of local government known as the township had no meeting for judicial purposes. When the hundred court assembled, it comprised all the freemen who were obliged to attend. Judgment was given upon the basis of the proofs adduced by the parties. Learned judges did not preside nor legal practitioners argue at these tribunals. The machinery of the court was set in motion and the course leading to a judgment was largely

[2] *Ancient Laws and Institutes of England*, ed. B. Thorpe (London, 1840), pp. 26–7.
[3] F. Pollock, *Expansion of the Common Law* (London, 1904), pp. 139–58.

determined by the parties to a controversy. Judicial procedure in the hundred court represented a somewhat frail substitution of orderly forms of justice for the settlement of disputes by private vengeance.

Royal power was established in England following the migration, although strong kingship did not arise until the time of Alfred. But already the folkmoot of the hundred had been supplemented by the county court. Neither of these courts was a king's court, although the king might supervise to some degree their activities. Royal authority was present in the county court in the person of the sheriff, and the king might inquire into the administration of justice in any part of the realm. He could not, however, interfere with the decisions of the popular courts. Finally, there was always the court of the king assisted by his council of wise men, the Witan, from whom justice could be sought when, after due diligence, it could not be obtained in the hundred or county courts.

Procedure among the Anglo-Saxons, as in all primitive legal systems, was characterized by extreme formalism and rigidity. Mistakes in form by either party were generally fatal in any controversy. The truth or falsity of a claim was not determined by anything resembling modern rules of evidence. There was rather an appeal to the supernatural. The simplest of these forms was the oath supported by oath helpers, who testified not to the facts in the case but to the truth of the oath. The procedural rules were limited to the number of oath helpers to be required. If an accused person was unable to clear himself by oath, he had to resort to one of the forms of ordeal.[4] The ordeal was an appeal to the judgment of God, and depended for its efficacy upon influences which sway the individual because of their hold on his emotional nature. The ordeal of hot iron might be sustained by the innocent where the guilty would fail. At least that was the belief. In any event, the ordeal as a method of proof continued in use until the Fourth Lateran Council in 1215 forbade the clergy to assist in the pro-

[4] The ordeal is fully described in H. C. Lea, *Superstition and Force* (Philadelphia, 1866), Ch. 3.

ceedings. Trial by combat, or wager of battle, came to England in the wake of the Norman Conquest. Although generally detested by the people, wager of battle by the twelfth century became the chief mode of trial in the king's court.[5]

The fundamental defect in Anglo-Saxon judicial administration was the almost total absence of executive authority. There is abundant evidence of the existence of institutions designed to substitute legal procedure for self-help. The feud was restricted by accepted rules, and money payments, or wergeld, replaced corporal revenge. The theft of cattle could be traced and a crude form of distress be invoked to obtain the return of a stolen animal. There arose a kind of ad interim possession while the outcome of a dispute over stolen cattle was awaited. Rights of ownership over land are scarcely mentioned in the Anglo-Saxon laws, and distinctions between contracts and torts are unknown. There was, however, an emerging distinction between injuries to an individual and offenses which endangered the security of the community. The latter early became cognizable before the king's courts where they could not be compensated by a money payment. Thus the foundations were laid for a genuine criminal law.

At the same time, there was little coercive power in the central government. Jurisdiction was seated in the consent of the parties rather than the compulsion of the state. A contumacious defendant in England could be dealt with no more effectively than among the Salian Franks. The fruits of judgment had to be gathered by the successful party himself. This he could often do only by waging war upon his adversary. What was lacking was a strong centralized government empowered not only to maintain a judicial authority but also to enforce its judgments. This lack was supplied in 1066 when William of Normandy made his conquest of England.[6]

[5] The literature on the wager of battle is not extensive. A good account will be found in G. Neilson, *Trial by Combat* (Glasgow, 1890), pp. 1–73. A brief statement is contained in F. A. Inderwick, *The King's Peace* (London, 1895). Typical appeals are set forth in *Select Pleas of the Crown* (Selden Society Publications, ed. F. W. Maitland, Vol. I, London, 1888).
[6] Pollock and Maitland, I, Bk. I, Ch. 2.

REFORMS OF THE NORMAN CONQUERORS

The Normans before coming to England had given convincing demonstrations of their genius for administration. It was fortunate that William I and his followers possessed administrative skills, for they brought to England less law then they found there. Their task was that of adapting the customary law of the Anglo-Saxons to the exigencies of a new regime which they were about to establish. William I wished to exchange his position of poor Norman duke for that of rich English king. He was also eager to capitalize on the threadbare fiction that he was heir to the kingdom of Edward the Confessor by lawful succession. William I, therefore, found it easy to promise the people whom he had subjected that he would respect their ancient laws. To these he added sparingly by legislation.

The situation which confronted the Norman conquerors was greatly confused by the multiplicity of local rules and customs. Custom is nothing but practice, and people behave differently in different communities. The result was that a legal act might be conditioned by varying rules in different parts of the realm. This was wholly unsatisfactory to a king who sought to become the ruler of a united people. The Normans could have brushed aside the Anglo-Saxon customary laws and imposed upon the conquered people legal rules of their own. But William I and his successors brought from the continent no legal system capable of replacing the native customary law. The only legal system which they could have imported was the Roman law, upon the recovery of which men were working at the time on the other side of the Alps. It is useless to speculate as to what would have happened in England if Roman law had been "received," as was done at a later date in Germany. The Norman conquerors followed another course; they reduced a myriad of local customs to single rules. That is to say, they created out of the materials which they found in England a common law for the whole of the realm.[7]

[7] *Ibid.*, Ch. 4.

Land law first occupied the attention of the new rulers of England. William I had promised the English who accepted the new regime the enjoyment of their ancient rights. He had also to reward his followers who by coming across the English Channel had made possible the Norman victory. There was also the Church which expected recognition for the part played by the clergy in support of the Norman claims. The only way these numerous and varied supporters of the Norman conquerers could be satisfied was through some form of landholding which would insure the maintenance of order at the same time that it contributed to the enrichment of the government. The nascent feudalism helped to accomplish both of these ends.

Feudal land law was brought by the application of the oath of fealty and the ceremony of homage to tenure in land. The vassal not only swore to render specific duties to his lord but also received guarantees from the lord that he might enjoy the land and its produce during his good behavior. The feudal relationship was therefore one in which rights and duties accrued to both parties. Feudalism was highly susceptible to the weakening of centralized government. William I could see what had happened to the empire of Charlemagne and guard against the same evil arising in England. The Norman conquerors therefore supplanted the complicated and unintelligible irregularities of the Anglo-Saxon land tenures with a simple and uniform feudal tenure. The king became the supreme landlord, and all private land was held mediately or immediately from him.[8]

At the same time, in the famous Council of Salisbury of 1086, the king exacted from "all the landowners of substance in England whose vassals soever they were" oaths of submission and allegiance. The Salisbury oath was not an integral part of the feudal system; it was rather a departure from it.[9] By providing a direct tie between the king and all freeholders, this oath was a precaution taken against

[8] W. Stubbs, *Constitutional History of England*, 3 vol., 6th ed. (London, 1903), Chs. 9, 11.

[9] *Ibid.*, pp. 289–90.

the disintegrating power of feudalism. The great achievement of William I was the introduction of an intelligent system of land-holding at the same time that the unity of the royal authority was maintained.

The royal officials in the twelfth and thirteenth centuries had other and not less important tasks to perform, in addition to the construction of a land law. They were also under the immediate necessity of building an adequate system of courts and improving the legal procedure. Before the Norman Conquest, the settlement of disputes was left almost entirely in the hands of the hundred and shire courts; recourse to the king was to be had only if justice could not be obtained in the local moots. The forms of procedure, as we have already seen, involved appeals to the supernatural and did not depend upon reason for their unfolding. By the middle of the twelfth century the time had arrived when the administration of justice must be confided to professional judges and the ancient forms of trial by oath and ordeal be supplanted by rational insti-tutions.[10] The kings of England were greatly helped in the work of judicial reform by the adaptation of the Norman inquest to provide a new form of trial.

INTRODUCTION OF THE JURY

The institution of trial by jury is now recognized to have been derived from the Norman inquest. It did not originate in ancient popular custom but in royal privilege. The vigorous royal power built up by the Frankish rulers included an institution, the inquest, for discovering the extent of the king's rights in the community, especially in fiscal matters. This required that the best and most trustworthy men in each community should assemble in the local court where they swore to the best of their knowledge and belief what lands and what rights should belong to the king in the district. In the beginning, the inquest was a form of administrative rather than judicial procedure, and although occasionally granted as a

[10] E. Jenks, *Short History of English Law*, Ch. 4.

privilege to the Church in order to protect Church lands, it continued to be the regular means whereby the Frankish kings evaded the technicalities and rigor of folk law in determining the rights of the crown. The extension of the inquest to judicial procedure in the ordinary courts of law was the later work of the Normans.

Introduced into England from Normandy soon after the Conquest, the sworn inquest was a prerogative procedure of the crown as it had been on the continent. But in the twelfth century it was extended by the king to his subjects.[11] In the *assize utrum* of 1164, Henry II decreed that a jury of twelve men should decide certain cases of conflict between the claims of the Church and those of the State. The establishment of trial by jury in civil cases was followed in 1166 by the Assize of Clarendon, which provided for indictment by local juries of accusation but which retained the ordeal for the trial of the chief cases.

The introduction of the trial jury in criminal cases did not occur until a somewhat later date. Although the Assize of Clarendon had specified the ordeal as the mode of trial, it is clear that by the beginning of the thirteenth century the jury was being used in criminal cases whenever the accused asked for it. The judges at this time apparently formed the habit of asking the accused whether he would submit to a trial by the country. In other words, he was asked to submit the question of his guilt or innocence to a second jury chosen from the neighbors present in the court. The submission was purely voluntary; a prisoner who refused to plead before such a tribunal could not be tried at all. He could, however, be subjected to the *peine forte et dure*, or judicial torture, in an attempt to compel him to plead. Prisoners sometimes died under the

---

[11] The literature on the jury system is abundant. The account of the origin of the jury by H. Brunner, *Die Entstehung der Schwurgerichte* (Berlin, 1872) is now generally accepted. Brunner's results form the basis for the treatment of the jury in Pollock and Maitland and in Holdsworth. See also J. B. Thayer, *Preliminary Treatise on Evidence at the Common Law* (Boston, 1898). Brunner's book has rendered obsolete the study of W. Forsythe, *History of Trial by Jury* (New York, 1875). An excellent account of the early Norman jury will be found in C. H. Haskins, *Norman Institutions* (Cambridge, Mass., 1918), Ch. 6.

torture, but since they had not been put on trial and had not been convicted they saved their property from confiscation. Their heirs at least benefited from their fortitude in choosing torture rather than trial by jury. Although this choice of alternatives continued until judicial torture was abolished in 1772, trial by jury in criminal cases became the usual mode of procedure in England during the thirteenth century.

REFORMS OF HENRY II

The great era of legal reform which began in the reign of Henry II saw the triumph of the king's courts. Through the use of the jury and by the promulgation of his assizes, the king was able to draw from the popular moots and the feudal courts cases to be heard before his judges. By the time Glanvil wrote his treatise in the late twelfth century the process by which the ancient customs off the country were to be transformed into the English common law was well under way.[12]

Henry II and his successors were careful not to impose upon the people new laws. The king was always under God and the law. But through his assizes, which were formal regulations directed to his officials for the conduct of the public business, the king was able to direct the course of judicial administration. Official practice therefore became a powerful agency not only in building up royal jurisdiction but also in shaping the law itself. In an age when new procedures must be devised for the interpretation and application of the law it is frequently difficult to distinguish clearly between law and procedure. The law sometimes appeared in different form in the decisions of the king's judges from what it had been in the local customs which were being supplanted. Sir Frederick Pollock has written:

We know that in the time of Henry I it was still possible to talk of district bodies of custom as existing in Wessex, in Mercia, and in the

[12] R. de Glanvil, *Tractatus de legibus et consuetudinibus regni Angliae*, ed. G. W. Woodbine (New Haven, 1932).

Danelaw; that in the time of Henry II there were still undefined varieties of usage . . . ; and that in the time of Henry III men spoke only of the laws and customs of England, and whatever did not conform to the common law as declared by the king's court had to justify itself as an exception on some special ground. The king's judges, and they alone, had power to lay down what the general custom of England, in other words the common law, for the terms are synonymous in our books, must be taken to be.[13]

In short, by the middle of the thirteenth century there existed an English common law by which the king himself admitted he was bound.

THE ENGLISH COMMON LAW

Bracton wrote his *Leges et Consuetudinibus Angliae* between 1250 and 1258, after England had passed through a serious constitutional crisis. The bad government which became the misfortune of England under the sons of Henry II was corrected in 1215 by the issuance of Magna Carta. This was a constitutional document of the greatest significance which proclaimed that the king is under the law. As a charter of liberties, every one of its provisions became the basis for future laws. Magna Carta laid the foundations for limitations upon governmental power among Englishmen wherever they might go. But from the point of view of the thirteenth century the great charter was a reaffirmation of the ancient rights which a lawless king had been setting aside. It was a legislative enactment, although no parliament then existed, in which the law of the land was proclaimed and the king agreed to abide by it. There was little that was new in Magna Carta, but it restored those imperishable rights which Henry II and earlier kings had clothed with the protection of the law.[14]

The growth of the English common law was threatened less by lawless kings than by the competition of the recovered Roman

[13] Pollock, p. 48.
[14] Stubbs, I, Ch. 1. See also W. S. McKechnie, *Magna Carta* (*Glasgow*, 1905).

law, and the canon law as applied in the ecclesiastical courts. The frivolities of Richard and the oppressive measures of John spelled bad government, but neither monarch weakened the law or its administration. On the contrary, the records show that the court at Westminster sat regularly and the itinerant justices visited the counties from time to time. John liked to travel about the country doing what he called justice, and taking with him a party of judges. In the midst of arbitrary and tyrannical government the law continued its sound course of development.

There arose, however, across the Alps in the twelfth century a revival of Roman law. Irnerius at Bologna between 1100 and 1130 laid the foundations for a study of Roman law which was continued by his pupils until it culminated in the Great Gloss of Accursius in the thirteenth century. The restored Corpus Juris of Justinian was studied and taught in England. Indeed, at the close of the twelfth century there was no more popular legal study at Oxford than the work of the civilians. Vacarius came from Italy to teach Roman law, some say at Oxford and others at London, and remained to become legal adviser to the Archbishop of York. From the reign of Stephen onwards, the study of both Roman and canon law continued to be pursued at Oxford and elsewhere in England. At the same time, many English clerics traveled to Italy, there to become doctors *utriusque iuris*. But in spite of all this intellectual activity, Roman law in England remained an academic discipline. It was attractive to men of learning "but it soon became plain that in England there would be no court administering Roman law, unless it were the court of a powerful university."[15]

[15] Pollock and Maitland, I, Bk. I, Ch. 5. The activities of the Bolognese glossators will be found described in most legal histories. See P. Vinogradoff, *Roman Law in Medieval Europe* (London, 1909), Ch. 2. An excellent account of Roman law in England is T. E. Scrutton, *The Influence of Roman Law on the Law of England* (Cambridge, 1885). An older account, now somewhat outmoded, is C. Guterbock, *Bracton and His Relation to the Roman Law*, tr. Brinton Coxe (Philadelphia, 1866). A comparison of some of the leading rules and institutions of the English and Roman systems will be found in W. W. Buckland and A. D. McNair, *Roman Law and Common Law*, 2nd ed. rev. by F. H. Lawson (Cambridge, 1952).

The real rival of the Roman law in England was the canon law, and the strongest opponents of the civilians were the canonists. From humble beginnings, a monk of Bologna had founded a school and laid the foundations of a mighty system of canon law. Gratian collected all the decretals of the popes down to the year 1139 in his Decretum and paved the way for the great collection published by Gregory IX in 1234. Copying the methods of Irnerius and the glossators, Gratian illuminated the canons of the Church and made of them a scientific and living body of law. In so doing, he and his followers drew heavily upon the Roman law; they were masters not only of church law but also of the civil law.

A broad jurisdiction over matters as well as parties was claimed in behalf of canon law. The Church, as we have already seen, gained control of all matrimonial causes and the law of inheritance came readily within its jurisdiction. Church courts claimed to enforce all promises made by oath or by pledge of faith. In the latter matter, Henry II came into rude conflict with Becket, Archbishop of Canterbury, and was victorious. Thereafter the king's courts rather than the ecclesiastical tribunals entertained most charges of breach of faith.[16]

With respect to parties, the Church asserted its right to deal with all persons who had been admitted to holy orders. This included clergymen and monks, together with a vast number of men in the lower echelons of the ecclesiastical hierarchy. The privilege known as benefit of clergy required that all persons in holy orders charged with crime be delivered to the church courts for trial. Penalties short of capital punishment could be imposed by the church courts. But in practice the transfer of a criminal case to an ecclesiastical tribunal on a plea of privilege was merely a prelude to the liberation of the accused.

The protection of the Church was given to all accused persons

[16] The growth of canon law is nowhere described in a way to interest students of jurisprudence. Holdsworth, and Pollock and Maitland will suffice for the beginner. See also F. W. Maitland, *Roman Canon Law in the Church of England* (London, 1898), and W. Ullmann, *Medieval Papalism; the Political Theories of the Medieval Canonists* (London, 1949).

in the right of sanctuary. In the institution known as the blood feud, a person being pursued might flee to the protection of church property where the clergy would safeguard him against the avenger of blood who was in pursuit.[17] Terms could then be made between the parties. While the right of sanctuary was a humane endeavor to regulate the rigors of the blood feud, it became a great nuisance when the state was supplanting self-help with orderly processes of criminal law. For a time the right of sanctuary lingered in the practice of abjuring the realm. The accused in the presence of the coroner confessed his crime and took an oath to quit the country never to return. He was then given safe conduct to some port whence he sailed for a foreign country. If he did not leave England promptly, or if he should return, he could at once be sentenced to death. In this way many criminals became outlaws and were sent doubtless to become troublers of the peace in other countries. The privilege of sanctuary yielded slowly to the increasing claims of state power, and it was not until 1623 that it was entirely abolished.

The ecclesiastical courts were comprised within a judicial system at the head of which was the papal curia at Rome. Appeals could be taken, and were encouraged to be taken, to the pope on all doubtful points of church law. The judges were ecclesiastics under the discipline of the Church who were bound to obey all papal decrees upon pain of being unfrocked. When, therefore, the popes in the decades preceding the time of Bracton attacked the teaching of Roman law, strict compliance with their orders followed. Honorius III in 1219 forbade the teaching of Roman law in the great theological school at the University of Paris and Innocent IV about 1254 is supposed to have decreed that the civilians should not be read in any country, except Italy and Germany, unless the

[17] There is an abundance of references to the blood feud in all histories of early legal institutions. Perhaps the best way to study this institution is to read *The Story of Burnt Njal*, 2 vol., ed. G. W. Dasent (Edinburgh, 1861). This stirring account of the administration of justice in Iceland during the tenth century is reprinted in Everyman's Library. See also E. Jenks, *Law and Politics in the Middle Ages* (New York, 1912), Ch. 4.

rulers of the countries should decide otherwise. English ecclesiastics could cheerfully obey the papal injunctions to abstain from reading the civilians, but they were unable to eschew the English law.

In the first place, the king's judges were nearly all churchmen. The office of justiciar was not held by a layman until the reign of Henry II, and down to a much later time the chancellor was nearly always an ecclesiastic. Although in the thirteenth century the king's justices came to be officially styled "justices learned in the law," the court was largely staffed by clergymen. Their theological training had given them knowledge of canon law, and through this had come an acquaintance with the methods of the civilians. In the second place, these men were frequently called upon to perform a dual function; they had to administer justice in the king's court at the same time that they were required to adjudicate in the church courts. What the justice learned in one court he could not forget in the other. Finally, the scientific precision imparted to both kinds of law by the doctors of Bologna was of inestimable value to the English justices in dealing with the legal data confronting them. The ancient laws and customs of the realm had to be woven into a system and there was no better, and perhaps no other, way for the justices and textbook writers to do this than to resort to the lessons to be learned from civilians and canonists.[18]

The English common law from the time of Henry II was never in danger of being supplanted by any other legal system. That is not to say, however, that those who shaped the law of England did not borrow heavily from both Roman and canon law. Terms and definitions were imported into England from the two systems of law, and upon occasion whole sets of rules, especially in the forms of procedure, came from Italy to enrich the English common law. In the time of Bracton the English law had not only maintained its integrity as an independent system but it had also taken from other systems whatever it required to give to its rules precision and clarity.

[18] Holdsworth, II, pp. 137–42, 227–9.

BRACTON AND HIS WORK

The work of Bracton has been called "the crown and flower of English medieval jurisprudence."[19] Certainly it became at once the leading textbook of English law. The work was copied by many medieval scribes, and there are in existence today almost fifty manuscripts. Epitomes were written, the best known being those of Britton and Fleta, textbook writers in the reign of Edward I. But it has not been until recent years that a satisfactory printed edition of Bracton has been made.

Bracton states that he is writing a Summa, but that he does not intend to follow the model set by the civilians. In other words, he does not plan to follow the tripartite division of the law of persons, things, and actions familiar to all students of the Roman law. Indeed, it is difficult to believe that Bracton had a definite plan for his work. The book was unfinished at the time of his death and he had already spent years in revising and interpolating passages in the writing he had done. There is an introduction which follows the tripartite division of Roman law somewhat closely, but this is a very small part of the whole treatise. Bracton never forgot that he was dealing with English law. The nature of his materials soon compelled him to abandon reliance upon Roman models and attempt an arrangement of his own.

The Roman materials Bracton took largely from the Summa of Azo, the leading glossator of the thirteenth century, although references are made to several parts of the Corpus Juris.[20] Whereas Glanvil had regarded the Roman as foreign law, Bracton seized

[19] Pollock and Maitland, I, Bk. I, p. 206. Bracton *De Legibus et consuetudinibus Angliae*, ed. G. E. Woodbine, 4 vol. (New Haven, 1915–42). This edition has rendered all the earlier editions of Bracton unserviceable. Holdworth, II, pp. 237–43, discusses the copies and epitomes of Bracton's book that were made in the lifetime of the author and immediately thereafter. The whole of the first volume of the Woodbine edition of Bracton deals with the MSS of the treatise and the use the editor has made of them.

[20] A comparison of passages in the work of Bracton and that of the glossator will be found in *Bracton and Azo* (Selden Society Publications, ed. F. W. Maitland, Vol. VIII, London, 1894).

upon the work of civilians and canonists alike to help him organize and explain the law of England. The greater part of the text shows slight trace of Roman influence, although Roman terms are occasionally used. When Bracton gets beyond his introduction and turns to the serious exposition of the English law, he appears to be fully aware that he is dealing with a legal system which is rapidly growing in his own day. The various kinds of jurisdiction within the kingdom are set forth, and the rules of procedure in an action are explained. Lengthy accounts of the more important assizes are given, and consideration of the writ procedure is begun. The writ of right is being explained when, for the last time, Bracton laid down his pen.

As might be expected of a man who spent much of his life on the bench, Bracton was greatly interested in procedure. He made extensive use of the plea rolls of some of the famous judges of the king's court. At the same time, he compiled a Note Book in which he collected numerous cases of the reign of Henry III.[21] In this, Bracton centered attention upon the importance of judicial precedent in the development of the law at the same time that he emphasized the dependence of substantive law upon the law of procedure. The citation of authorities which he began has been pursued throughout the long history of the English law. Modern reporting did not begin until the reign of Henry VIII, yet the Year Books from the time of Edward I not only tell of the development of the law but also give fascinating accounts of the day to day activities in court.[22] Case law has been the heart and soul of the common law.

EDWARD I AND LEGISLATION

When Edward I became king in 1272, legislation for the first time forged to the front as a method of developing the law.

[21] *Bracton's Note Book* has been edited by F. W. Maitland and published in three volumes (London, 1887).

[22] The Year Books profess to be reports of cases decided in the king's courts from the middle of the thirteenth to the middle of the sixteenth centuries. They are reprinted in the Publications of the Selden Society. An interesting account of the Year Books is given in Holdsworth, II, pp. 526–66.

Throughout the preceding years the royal tribunals had slowly but relentlessly triumphed over the old popular courts and the judicial institutions of feudalism, but at no time during the Middle Ages did the enacted law cover much ground. With Edward I, the statute came to perform a useful service. "The first place among the influences which shaped the development of law in Edward I's reign must be assigned to the Statute Book," wrote the leading historian of English law. "It would hardly be an exaggeration to say that we must wait for the nineteenth century until we can again assign to direct legislation upon matters legal so great an influence upon the technical development of the law."[23] It was the task of the king and his ministers to arrange and codify, "in such informal ways as the spirit of his age and country allowed, the legal system which had grown up in disorderly abundance in the previous generations."[24] As a result of his legislative activities, Edward I has been called the "English Justinian." The title is merited because the English king did precisely what the Roman emperor had done; he reduced to orderly form the law which he found, without adding to it by way of innovation.

In the time of Edward I, Parliament was not the great lawmaking body it has since become. Bracton speaks of "the counts and barons of the great court" as advisers to the king. He also says that if the king should seek to rule without the law, it shall be the duty of these same counts and barons "to put upon him the bridle of the law." Parliament in the time of Edward I declared but did not make the law. The great legislative acts of the reign, such as the Statutes of Westminster I and II, dealt with the whole field of law, although they added almost nothing new. Even when the definite and final scheme of Parliament was achieved in 1295, the members came to Westminster to approve or disapprove proposals of the king and not to initiate bills for his signature. "What touches all," ran Edward's writ of summons, "should be approved by all, and it is also clear that common dangers should be met by measures

[23] Holdsworth, II, p. 299.
[24] T. F. Tout, *Edward the First* (London, 1903), p. 122.

agreed upon in common."[25] Parliament was a court long before it became a legislature.

The growth of the legislative authority of Parliament was accompanied by a wider distribution of its judicial functions. From an early date, the issuance of writs whereby a man cited his adversary into court was the duty of the chancellor. He prepared the writs, which ran in the name of the king, and sold them at fixed prices. When it was proclaimed that no new writs should issue without the consent of Parliament, the law tended to become a commentary upon the existing writs. If a novel case arose, for which no writ was available, the matter was referred to the chancellor as the official who might be expected to do justice. To the ministerial duty of issuing common law writs, the chancellor had added the judicial function of deciding cases for which no remedy at law existed. He came to enjoy a jurisdiction all his own, where, in the name of equity and good conscience, he remedied defects of the common law.[26] The principles which guided him in the exercise of his judicial powers flowed for the most part from the common law, although he derived much help from the civilians and canonists. Thus the equity courts arose to supplement those of the common law. Litigants were expected to fulfill all the requirements of the law; but if justice were not then forthcoming, recourse could be had to the equitable jurisdiction of the court of chancery. The amount of business which poured into the equity courts was immense, and in time the procedures of the chancellor became as rigid and stereotyped as those of the law courts.

Meanwhile, the system of common law jurisdiction after the older local courts had decayed required the establishment of new royal tribunals. The plea rolls of the thirteenth century show a distinction between the court which met at a certain place to hear

[25] See C. H. McIlwain, *The High Court of Parliament and Its Supremacy* (New Haven, 1910), p. 21. This historical essay on the boundaries between legislation and adjudication in England gives an excellent account of the growth of Parliament and its relation to the common law.

[26] The history of the court of chancery will be found in Holdsworth, I, Ch. 5.

common pleas and the court which followed the king, with jurisdiction over common pleas and pleas of the crown. Before the
middle of the century the distinction was complete, and the court
of common pleas was established to sit at a fixed place, usually at
Westminster. The court-held *coram rege* in the fourteenth century
became the king's bench to hear criminal causes and other pleas of
the crown.

The court of exchequer was an outgrowth of the financial administration of the country, and for more than two hundred and
fifty years was limited almost entirely to the hearing of revenue
cases. The itinerant justices who rode the circuits in Bracton's time
ultimately became integral parts of the system of common law
jurisdiction. Finally, the justices of the peace, who were commis-
sioned by the crown, became the conservators of the peace in the
counties. Their duties have been many and varied and have embraced administration as well as judicature. The judicial structure
erected in piecemeal fashion in England towards the close of the
Middle Ages remained in broad outline unchanged until the enactment in 1873 of the Judicature Act.

The growth of Parliament as a legislative body meant that statutes in matters small and large came to influence the development
of the law. At Rome, as we have already seen, the need for legislation was never great. During the republican period the praetor at
first assisted, then supplemented, and finally boldly corrected the
civil law. In England, men came to look upon Parliament as the
authority which was to correct the common law. The judges might
occasionally complain that some act of Parliament was directly
at variance with the common law, but the act was obeyed none-
theless. The omnipotence of Parliament, about which Blackstone
was later to write,[27] brought the common law under the superin-
tendence of statutory law. The courts as well as the laws which
they enforced depended upon the will of the English people as
reflected in the acts of their Parliament.

[27] *Blackstone's Commentaries,* ed. Chase (New York, 1877), p. 15.

VII

Systems of National Law

SYSTEMS OF NATIONAL LAW, except in England, did not arise before the nineteenth century.[1] Local and provincial customs existed in abundance throughout western Europe. Feudal law, canon law, and the law merchant supplied somewhat uniform rules with respect to the matters with which each dealt in all continental countries. But the only common law on the continent was the Roman law. When the Corpus Juris of Justinian was revived by the medieval studies at Bologna and elsewhere in Italy, the Roman law became subsidiary law for nearly all continental countries. In other words, the rules of the civilians could be cited in the courts only when local law was unavailing. Roman law was secondary law; local law in a vast number of jurisdictions had priority over this

[1] For an account of continental systems of law, see *A General Survey of Events, Sources, Persons and Movements in Continental Legal History* (Boston, 1912). The private law of France has been discussed by J. Brissaud, *A History of French Private Law* (Boston, 1912). For an account of Italian law, see C. Calisse, *A History of Italian Law* (London, 1928). The best history of German law is that by H. Brunner, *Deutsche Rechtsgeschichte*, 2 vol. (2nd ed. rev. Munich-Leipzig, 1928). A history of German law in English translation is that of R. Huebner, *History of Germanic Private Law*. tr. Philbrick. (Boston, 1912).

127

common law. Nevertheless, the Roman law "was generally described and, until it was superseded by modern national codifications, it continued to be described as the 'common law' of continental Europe."[2]

The foundations of modern continental systems of law must be sought in the work of Irnerius and his school at Bologna in the twelfth century. Their restoration of the law books of Justinian made possible the extension of Roman law to France, Germany, and other European countries. The work of the glossators was one of pure scholarship, but teaching as well as research was included among their tasks. Doctors of both kinds of law made their way through western Europe carrying with them manuscripts of the Corpus Juris, or summaries of its contents, as well as the Decretum of Gratian and the canons of the church. From these they gave instruction to all who were willing to pay their fees. For a time, in the reign of Stephen, the teaching of Roman law was forbidden in England, but elsewhere in Europe the civilians had a clear field in the universities.[3]

The task of adapting the Roman law to the requirements of the courts fell to other hands. The glossators did no more than expound the law as it had existed six hundred years earlier. For them, Justinian was still living and legislating; with the needs of their own generation they had no interest. But the commentators who followed in the fourteenth century had practical ends in view. Under the leadership of Cino of Pistoia the writing of commentaries was begun in which the ancient principles of the Roman texts were applied to the Germanic and feudal customs. The work was continued by Bartolus of Sassoferrato, who was interested especially in harmonizing the Roman law and the statutes of the Italian cities. Although the writings of Bartolus continued to be studied and quoted for two hundred years, the commentators were subjected to severe criticism. Their treatises were charged with a certain amount of insipidity, which would appear to be justified. At the

[2] Munroe Smith, *Development of European Law* (New York, 1928), p. 258.
[3] See P. Vinogradoff, *Roman Law in Medieval Europe* (London, 1909).

precise moment when many men were turning in disgust from the law, Alciat opened new vistas to legal studies by linking them with the new humanism then growing up. A genuine Italian law might have resulted if Alciat had not in 1518 accepted a call to Avignon, where he transplanted his method to French soil. The methods of Bartolus and the commentators became old-fashioned as Alciat made Bourges the center of the new legal learning. Italy lost by the emigration of Alciat but France gained.

GROWTH OF LAW IN FRANCE

The school at Bourges was not content with illuminating the text of Justinian's books; they wished to reconstruct what the emperor had discarded. The writings of Papinian, Ulpian, Paulus, and the other jurisconsults which had not been included in the Digest were to be restored for the use of scholars. The leadership in this extraordinary enterprise was taken by Cujas, who became easily the most distinguished member of the faculty at Bourges. It has been said "that if all the rest of the world's labors on Roman law were to disappear, those of the French school would suffice to preserve its treasures for our use."[4]

The school of Cujas was not, however, without its opponents. The followers of Bartolus, who continued to hold their own in Italy, made important converts in France. Bodin wrote that when he was only a teacher of law he despised the Bartolists, but he thought differently after the experience of practical work. The same may be recorded of other men. The practitioners of the law were less satisfied with the historical and theoretical studies of Cujas than they were with the fundamentalism of Bartolus. Albericus Gentilis, who shares with Hugo Grotius the credit for the founding of modern international law, was a Bartolist. Gentilis was an Italian who sought political sanctuary in England, where

[4] See the essay by F. W. Maitland, "English Law and the Renaissance," *Select Essays in Anglo-American Legal History* (Boston, 1907), I, pp. 168–207.

he became regius professor of civil law at Oxford and also practiced in the admiralty court. The story is pretty much the same everywhere; Bartolus never lost his hold upon the courts, although the new humanism of Cujas and his school captured the imagination of the teachers and writers of the law. This might be expected, for Bartolus was a public official at Todi at the same time that he was the greatest commentator of his day.[5]

France was moving in the direction of a unified national law. As early as the first half of the sixteenth century, Charles Dumoulin dreamed of a single French code which would embrace the whole of customary law. Although nothing came of the dream, Colbert, the great financial minister of Louis XIV, in the next century made codifications of portions of the law at the same time that he improved the administration of justice. But it was not until Pothier in the eighteenth century produced his treatises on the civil law that a code of national law was foreshadowed. Pothier was a prodigious worker who served for fifty years on the bench while teaching law at Orleans. His twenty-six separate treatises cover the whole civil law. Among these are systematic treatises upon each title of the Digest and an extraordinary study of the law of obligations. Although Pothier was not an original thinker, his books did much to prepare the way for the composition of the Code Napoleon. With this great work France came to have a genuine system of national law.[6]

The late development of a system of national law in France can be explained on historical grounds. Before the thirteenth century customary law was observed in all the regions of France. In the south, the customs were derived in the main from the Breviary of Alaric and other Roman sources. It was therefore an easy task to

[5] An excellent monograph on Bartolus and his work is that by C. N. S. Woolf, *Bartolus of Sassoferrato* (Cambridge, 1913). See also J. N. Figgis, *Divine Right of Kings*, 2nd ed. (Cambridge, 1922, pp. 343 ff. for the influence of Bartolus on Gentilis and the founders of modern international law.

[6] For the history of French law and institutions before 1789, see F. Olivier-Martin, *Histoire du Droit Français des Origines* à la *Révolution* (Paris, 1948) and P. Viollet, *Histoire du Droit Civil Français*, 3rd ed. (Paris, 1905).

substitute the Corpus Juris for local usages in parts of France from Auvergne to the Mediterranean. These became the *pays du droit écrit* in which the legal writers as well as the courts employed the Roman law in the application and interpretation of the local customs.

In the northern provinces of France, known as the *pays coutumiers*, the customary law was largely Germanic in origin. It was not put in written form until the thirteenth century, when private compilations began to appear. The *Grand coutumier* of Normandy, which was compiled between 1270 and 1275, was one of the most remarkable legal works of the Middle Ages, distinguished alike for its lucidity and its methodical arrangement. Courts of record appeared in the north of France as early as the twelfth century. Within the next hundred years the Parliament of Paris sat as a supreme court to which appeals could be taken from all the northern provinces. Judicial decisions began to supplement the customary law, and royal courts with appellate jurisdiction were established in almost every region of France. In these courts, where local and provincial customs were silent, the Roman law as set forth by Justinian was applied.

Royal legislation came somewhat tardily, but effectively, to aid the development of the law. During the last two centuries of the monarchy, the ordinances of the king did much to reform the private law at the same time that they helped to create the conditions which led to the revolution. The storm which burst over France in 1789, and which destroyed the monarchy, was directed against special privileges designed to benefit certain persons and their lands. When the revolution was over, the public law, including the provisions for judicial administration, had been greatly altered, but the private law remained much as it had been under the old regime. Every trace of special privilege was erased from the law, which meant that more equalitarian provisions in landholding and greater safeguards to individual freedom were introduced. Property rights were reorganized and the law of inheritance was relieved of many incumbrances. But the common customary law of France as modified by the Roman law and recorded in judicial decisions, together with such parts of the royal legislation as were congenial to the people, stood as the foundations of a national legal system. The military dictatorship of Napoleon was required to weld the conflicting interests to produce the famous code to which his name is attached.

SLOW LEGAL DEVELOPMENT IN GERMANY

Meanwhile, in Germany, centuries of legal development had failed to produce a system of national law. It has been frequently assumed that the reception of Roman law in 1495 by the judges of the Reichskammergericht ousted the customary law and established the law books of Justinian as the law for the whole of Germany. The true story is not so simple. In the first place, the reception was not that of Justinian's law books, but the judicial law elaborated in Italy based upon the Corpus Juris but subjected to many transformations by the commentators. In the second place, the customary law, although shoved aside and disdainfully neglected by the learned jurists of the canon and civil laws, retained a popular appeal in Saxony and some other parts of Germany. Finally, the stupid and superficial manner in which the jurists sought to apply the Roman law in disregard and defiance of local German usage led to a reaction which hindered the development of a genuine national law.

The action taken by the imperial high court of justice in 1495 was less revolutionary than would appear at first glance.[7] For more than two hundred years before this date, Roman law had been regarded as having subsidiary force in Germany. The theory of continuous empire, which was generally accepted both in Germany and Italy, regarded the kings of Germany as the successors to the Roman emperors. Frequent appeals to the Roman law by German

[7] The literature on the "reception" of Roman law in Germany is abundant. Among the leading books are W. Modderman, *Die Reception des römischen Rechts* (Jena, 1875) and C. A. Schmidt, *Reception des romischen Rechts in Deutschland* (Rostock, 1868).

rulers strengthened the notion that the Roman law was binding upon all subjects of the Holy Roman emperor. Roman law possessed a claim to validity in Germany, which the Hohenstaufen emperors did not overlook in their conflicts with the papacy. Unfortunately, neither the Hohenstaufens nor their successors possessed sufficient authority to unify the German principalities or to undertake legal reform. Jurisdiction belonged to the territorial rulers or, in the free cities, to the councils. There did not exist in Germany the centralized power of the crown which was the decisive factor in the development of the English common law. Particularism stood as a barrier to the invigoration of the imperial power as the highest legal authority within the empire.

Nevertheless, the territorial princes wished to improve the administration of justice. They called to their aid the learned doctors of canon and civil laws. The first of these received their training in Italy; a doctorate from one of the Italian universities became a prerequisite to appointment in church and secular courts. When German universities were founded in the fourteenth century, the teaching of canon and Roman law was promptly introduced. Thereafter, from Prague, Heidelberg, and the other German universities, graduates came forth to claim positions requiring a knowledge of the law. Judges and advocates trained in the writings of canonists and civilians comprised a learned profession.

This trained class of officials remained faithful to their civilian education. To them, the Roman law comprised the legal wisdom of the ages. When they got hold of the administration of justice, these men began to draw up contracts, testaments, and other documents according to the principles of Roman law. The popular courts were invaded by men of learning who refused to invoke the German law. Since very little had been done, or could be done, to place the German law in writing, the old customs were soon reduced to local usages which had to be proved in the courts. As the German law was superseded by the more precise and scientific rules of the civilians, a great deal of undeserved scorn was heaped upon the customary law. Judges and counsel alike termed the German law

133

jus barbarum, unworthy of confidence or respect. To some extent this affront to German law was encouraged by the territorial rulers, who believed that by giving their support to the Roman law they might draw to themselves something of the grandeur of imperial Rome.

The reception of Roman law was not to the liking of everybody in Germany. A proletarian revolution, undoubtedly stemming from the teachings of John Hus long after the reformer had been burned at the stake by order of the Council of Constance, was directed not only against the Roman law but also against all secular law. Other protests were more temperate and more directly aimed at the foreign law which was replacing the old customs. Some complained that rights were less secure than they had been in earlier days. Others lamented the passing of old usages which were more congenial to the common man than the rules of the Corpus Juris. But the harshest criticism was levelled at the legal profession.[8]

Lawyers were unknown to the popular courts of the Salian Franks. The *schöffen,* or lay-judges, were often shrewd but none of them had received scientific legal training. Litigation was conducted by the parties to the action and was free. When professional lawyers began to represent the parties, and to argue in a language unknown to the people, they necessarily charged a fee. Compensation for legal services would have incurred no hostility if all the lawyers had been well trained. But a legal education was costly, and many persons sought admission to practice with only a scanty knowledge of the law. Perhaps the deepest causes of dissatisfaction were the venal and corrupt practitioners who plundered their clients and created intolerable delays in the administration of the law from which they alone could profit. It is significant that many modern expressions of contempt for the legal profession were first heard in sixteenth century Germany.

The philosophers were the first to rescue the law from the stag-

[8] See R. von Stintzing, *Geschichte der deutschen Rechtswissenschaft,* 3 vol. (Munich and Leipzig, 1880–1910).

nation into which it had fallen in Germany by the time of the Thirty Years' War. The publication by Grotius of his *De jure belli ac pacis* in 1625 did not at first attract much attention in Germany. But before the close of the century, German legal science at the hands of Samuel Pufendorf was brought into close association with the natural law tradition implanted in the work of Grotius.[9] Although Pufendorf is usually considered as one of the founders of modern international law, his voluminous writings range over the various fields of public and private law. He adheres somewhat closely to Roman law but does not hesitate to quote the capitularies of Frankish kings and the customs of Teutonic peoples when these best serve his purpose.

To his great contemporary Leibnitz, the work of Pufendorf appeared unrealistic and pedestrian. Leibnitz regarded the science of law as embracing "a knowledge of things divine and human," as the Roman jurisconsults had done. He entered public employment at Mainz, but never permitted his public duties seriously to interfere with his studies or his writing. The great contribution of Leibnitz lies in the constant pressure which he exerted in his writing and in personal relations in favor of codification and legal reform. He recognized that such reform through imperial legislation was impossible, and he did not disdain to appeal to the territorial rulers to undertake the task each within his own particular jurisdiction. The Prussian code of 1794 is traceable directly to the influence of Leibnitz.

It was, however, in the work of Herman Conring that legal science secured a national basis.[10] The deep insight of Conring into the scientific tendency of his time led him to see that a national law for his country must be the result of a Roman law which was transformed by German thought. In other words, there must be a revival of the study of German law; a knowledge of Roman law

[9] Much of the important writing of Pufendorf is available in English. See Classics of International Law, vol. X, XV (Oxford, 1927, 1931).

[10] The work of Conring has not been studied extensively outside Germany. An account of his work will be found in E. von Moeller, *Hermann Conring, der Vörkämpfer des deutschen Rechts* (Hanover, 1915).

alone could not fit anybody for legal practice. The academic study of German law was urged at the close of the seventeenth century by Thomasius, whose pupil Georg Beyer gave the first university lectures on the subject a few years later. With Beyer, the German law received a systematic treatment, separate from the Roman, in the classroom and in textbooks.

All this activity was far from creating a system of national law. There was still lacking the historical knowledge necessary to penetrate Roman antiquities or German customs and usages in the past. Moreover, the empire was deteriorating so steadily that there was no authority sufficiently powerful to unify the territorial principalities. The elector of Brandenberg after the Thirty Years' War took the lead in the formation of a political center around which a new German empire was later to be formed, but this was not accomplished until the nineteenth century. Meanwhile, the Holy Roman empire was completely dissolved by Napoleon, and the legal disunity of Germany was obvious to everybody. Once again the philosophers, aided by the historians, came to the rescue of German law and legal institutions.

Immanuel Kant at the university in Königsberg during the turmoil attending the revolution in France put forth the most forceful exposition of the theory of natural law in modern times. The Kantian system captured the imagination of many men, but it relied too much upon Roman law to satisfy German nationalists. Hegel, the great philosopher whose academic career was almost wholly wrecked by the Napoleonic invasion of Germany, turned to the study of German antiquities and found them adequate for his philosophy of history. A national spirit was awakened which has continued to exist to the present day, and which has compelled a complete revision of previous notions of the part to be played by Roman law in the legal system of Germany.

Controversy over a national code for Germany began in 1814 and continued almost to the end of the century. The first jurist to urge a code was Anton F. J. Thibaut, professor of Roman law at Heidelberg, who published a pamphlet entitled "On the Necessity of a General Civil Code for Germany" in 1814. In this work, Thibaut deplores the condition of legal disunity then existing in Germany, which he traces to the adoption of Roman law in piecemeal fashion by the different territorial rulers. At the same time, the whole of native law was so imperfect that recourse must be had constantly to the alien code. The only remedy, according to Thibaut, is the immediate adoption of one general code, written in the German language and eliminating all foreign law, including the Roman, as unsuited to the needs of modern Germany. To this proposal Savigny, the greatest German jurist of the early nineteenth century, replied in a pamphlet entitled "The Vocation of Our Times for Legislation and Jurisprudence." Savigny's contention was that a people develops its own law in much the same way that it does its language and social customs. If it borrows from an alien law in order to cure disorder among popular customs and to give scientific precision, this is done by the jurists in much the same way that a philologist enriches a language by borrowing from other tongues the words which he requires. Savigny was therefore unalterably opposed to any codification which did not rest upon the historic monuments of the law through which the people had progressed.

The views of Savigny and the historical school of jurisprudence prevailed. They not only routed for a time the advocates of immediate codification but also helped to overthrow the predominance of natural law in theories of law and politics. Tension among German legal scholars lessened after 1848 and fears of codification subsided. Men began to perceive that both German and Roman law had contributed a great deal to the legal system under which the German people were living. The inadequacies of the existing law arose not because it stemmed from Roman or Teutonic sources but because there did not exist in all of Germany a central government powerful enough to establish national unity. This defect was left for the Franco-Prussian war to cure. When German arms emerged triumphant after the battle of Sedan, the way was clear to proclaim the new German Empire. Under the leadership of

Prussia, a strong central government was established in Germany and the formation of a German code was begun.

THE CODE OF NAPOLEON

Codification may be said to be the permanent result of the Napoleonic dictatorship on the continent of Europe. Certainly Napoleon regarded the code as his greatest gift to France. "Nothing," he wrote at St. Helena, "can blot out my Civil Code. That will live eternally."[11] But the compilation of codes was not confined to France; similar codifications were undertaken elsewhere in Europe and even in Latin America when countries in the western hemisphere gained their independence. Many of the modern codes formally reflect the Roman models, but nowhere exhibit a slavish copying of Roman law in their contents. In other words, modern codes in each country where they have been adopted mark the culmination of a long period of legal development. Customs and usages of the people combine with rules of the Corpus Juris as interpreted by judges and textbook writers to form the pattern of each system of national law.

Napoleon gave to France five codes, of which the civil code was the most important. Its importance derived less from the driving force of Napoleon, who presided at many of the drafting sessions, than from the careful advance preparations made for its adoption. A commission of four members was appointed as early as August 13, 1800, among whom the preliminary work was divided. Portions of the code were completed in 1803, and were voted and put into force as they were made ready. The entire code of 2,281 articles was enacted on March 21, 1804. The remaining codes were enacted during the Napoleonic empire, but none of them was as successful as the civil code to which the name of Napoleon has been permanently attached.

[11] For an account of the civil code, see *Code Civil: Livre du Centenaire* (Paris, 1904) and J. Van Kan, *Les Efforts de Codification en France* (Paris, 1929).

The Code Napoleon comprised three books, each of which was subdivided into titles, and under each title was arranged the appropriate subjects. The principal sources utilized in the compilation were the customs of the northern provinces of France, the Roman law, the royal ordinances which had survived the destruction of the old regime, and portions of the revolutionary legislation. Throughout the code, the spirit of the customary law prevailed, which was not surprising since most of Napoleon's ministers came from the *pays coutumiers*. The influence of Napoleon Bonaparte can be discerned in some sections of the code, especially in the harsh treatment accorded to foreigners and the favorable consideration given to veterans after discharge from military service. Happily, the civil code was enacted at the precise moment in the history of France when its success could be best assured.

The Code Napoleon accompanied the victorious armies of France as they swept over the continent of Europe. The territories which Napoleon caused to be embraced within the French republic before the peace of Amiens in 1802 received the code at the same time it was enacted at Paris. Later it was extended to Italy, Holland, and the Hanseatic towns. Some of the German principalities and the kingdom of Sardinia adopted the code before it could be imposed upon them. Before the ultimate defeat of Napoleon, his code came to enjoy an authority and a jurisdiction greater than that of any body of law since the supremacy of the Roman empire.

The defeat of France and the exile of Napoleon checked the fortunes of the code. In some states it was repudiated and in others it was changed. But the movement for codification continued in high gear throughout the nineteenth century. The new republics of South America, as they were freed from the rule of Spain, copied the Code Napoleon. In widely separated countries of western Europe the code was imitated or utilized in some fashion to frame systems of national law. Only the Anglo-Saxon countries have preserved their law in the form of judicial decisions embodying the customary law and the statutes amendatory of the common law.

Elsewhere national law has been embodied in codes. This solution of the problem of obtaining a national law through legislation has been necessitated because no country in Europe, except England, could have afforded the time to create a legal system through the slow process of judicial decision.

CODES VERSUS COMMON LAW

The relative merits of a code struck off by legislation and a common law built by judicial decisions have been the subject of much controversy.[12] The debate must be endless while the contestants differ in the grounds of their arguments. The advantages and disadvantages of each system of law can be spun out in discussions without touching the fundamental question of which system offers the best means for the further development of the law. If codification introduces a set of rules wholly congenial to the life and spirit of the people for whom the code is intended, and at the same time insures the further development of the law, it would be highly desirable to ask the legislature to enact a code. On the other hand, if the adoption of a code involves forcing upon the people a set of foreign rules with recourse only to the legislature for their amendment, codification must be deplored. The solution of this problem must be sought in the legal history of each country.

Continental Europe from the fifth century onward depended increasingly upon codes. The general or common law was gradually destroyed by local codes which were ultimately replaced by national codes. Customs, when reduced to writing, appeared as codes, first in the private compilations undertaken in the thirteenth century and later in royal codifications. Throughout the centuries in which continental codes were being constructed, different causes

[12] The controversy over the adoption of a code in the State of New York is reflected in David Dudley Field, *Speeches, Arguments, and Miscellaneous Papers*, 3 vol. (New York, 1884–1890), I, pp. 307–483, and Munroe Smith, "State Statute and Common Law," *Political Science Quarterly* (II, pp. 105–134, III, pp. 134–164). Reprinted in *A General View of European Legal History*, pp. 52–109.

underlay the codification movement. In Italy the intense patriotism displayed in Machiavelli's *Prince* demanded a national law, although this was denied until 1865. German trade and commerce languished for more than two hundred years while local codes set up commercial laws which hindered national economic development. The diversity of customs in France precluded any unity of law for the nation until the revolution swept away all evidences of particularism. In each of these countries the lack of strong centralized government prevented the formation of a system of national law.

In England the situation was otherwise. When the Normans possessed themselves of the country in 1066, they found there a body of law superior to that which existed in Normandy. With the genius for administration which characterized the Normans, William I and his successors began to transform the Anglo-Saxon customs into a common law for the realm. This task fell to the king's judges, whose decisions, unless modified by statute, became the law. The judges were aided by a strong legal fraternity trained in the English law. The Inns of Court, which were guilds of lawyers with their apprentices, appeared early in the fourteenth century and provided a form of legal education which has continued to the present day. With a professionalized bench and bar backed by the power of the crown, the English common law was soon firmly established.

The Roman law as developed during the period of the empire had some striking similarities with the common law. These similarities are in method rather than content. "It may be a paradox, but it seems to be the truth," wrote Professor Buckland, "that there is more affinity between the Roman jurist and the common lawyer than there is between the Roman jurist and his modern civilian successor."[13] Both proceeded from case to case seeking to establish a good working set of rules and did not, like the modern civilian, regard the law as a set of rules to be deduced from a group of pri-

[13] W. W. Buckland, and A. D. McNair, *Roman Law and Common Law,* 2nd ed. rev. (Cambridge, 1952), p. xiv.

mary principles. It would be a mistake to think that Roman law had the same character as the civil law of modern Europe. The real Roman law is not to be found in the textbooks such as the Institutes of Gaius and Justinian but in the orderly writings of the jurists codified in the Digest of Justinian.[14] These are the living law derived from the contemplation of cases which arose in the courts.

The rejection of codification does not mean the denial of legislation. The statute has been utilized to assist, supplement, and correct the common law and thereby prevent stagnation in the legal system. The certainty which is inherent in a judicial decision is strengthened when subjected to legislative treatment. At the same time, greater flexibility is frequently attained for a rule of common law when the legislature extends its scope to matters not contemplated by the courts. Finally, the skill of the legislator may be required to brush aside rules of the common law which can no longer be reconciled with the actual conditions of life within the community.

Informed policy-making is the primary responsibility of a legislature. Whether this involves the alteration of existing law or the formulation of new rules of law, there will always be a political basis for an act of legislation. That is to say, a proposal to alter existing law or to frame a new law must be considered amid the shifting currents of opinion among contending legislators. Tactics are bound to play an important role in legislation. James Madison regarded legislation as the determination on an enlarged scale of issues which might otherwise be left to judicial decision. "What," he asked, "are many of the most important acts of legislation, but so many judicial determinations, not indeed concerning the rights of single persons, but concerning the rights of large bodies of citizens? And what are the different classes of legislators but advocates and parties to the causes which they determine?"[15] It is therefore important that the legislative function be performed by men who

[14] F. H. Lawson, *A Common Lawyer Looks at the Civil Law* (Ann Arbor, 1955), p. 75.
[15] *Federalist*, No. 10.

are as well informed as those who exercise the judicial powers.

Modern legislation has achieved its most significant successes where the legislators proceed upon a sound foundation of accumulated information. Conclusive and mouth-filling phrases no longer serve to formulate the public policies of people in a complex world. Nor can public policy be made to rest upon a priori assumptions from supposed principles of human nature. In order to solve the problems of modern states, legislators must have at hand reference libraries, research assistance, and bill-drafting facilities. From the factual knowledge thus obtained, the legislator is enabled to determine all the aspects of a problem. Of course, his vote will in the end be dictated by political considerations, but he cannot plead that he is uninformed.

In some jurisdictions, agencies known as legislative councils have been established with authorization to prepare and recommend programs of legislation to the legislative bodies. Legislative councils with power to recommend legislative programs are found in about twenty-three states in the United States. These agencies have not been uniformly successful and in many states have been vigorously opposed. They have been criticized as setting up a super-legislature. Members of a legislature are quite properly jealous of their rights and privileges. They resent interference with their freedom of action to introduce legislation beneficial to their constituents. This freedom of action is necessarily curtailed if recommended bills are given priority over other measures in the legislature. Agencies which seek merely to supply factual data are not open to this criticism. They do not impair the freedom of action of the legislator, because he alone determines how the results of investigation and research are to be used.

Public policy, in order to find embodiment in legislation, must be put in form for treatment by the legislature. In other words, a proper bill must be drafted if a valid statute is to result. Constitutional requirements must be scrupulously observed as well as the rules of procedure in the legislative body. But it should be remembered that legislation is a political act and perfection in statute-making is well-nigh impossible. The legislative draftsman dare not disregard the formal requirements of a bill, but he cannot be expected to foresee the changes which his draft may undergo in order to meet approval by the legislature. The legislative draftsman must frequently be satisfied with less than he could give to a bill in both content and style. It has been said that the choice between the second best and nothing at all is the normal situation. But this is a choice which the bill drafter must make, for his toil is unavailing if his work is not acceptable to a majority in the legislature.

No final answer can be given to the question which system, code or common law, is superior. Too much depends upon the way in which each arose in the country of its adoption. Italy presents a striking example of the endurance of a legal system which has its roots in the distant past. Codification is endemic to the Italians. They have always known, since the time of the XII Tables, no other system of law. Although the Code Napoleon was for a time imposed upon the country, Italy soon emerged to form a code of its own. Some of its provisions were derived from the French system, but the basic notions of the code existed long before the conquest of Italy by Napoleon. Changes in the code of 1865 have been made readily, conforming to the social and economic growth of the country. No other legal system would have been possible in Italy.

The extension of the common law to all English-speaking countries, on the other hand, has given abundant evidence of the vitality of a legal system built by judicial decisions. Codification is available within the common law to reduce to statutory form whatever rules appear to have become finally settled. Too much should not be attempted, because rules which rest upon decisions are withdrawn from the control of the courts when they become statutory. Where it is wholly feasible to codify the law merchant in the law of negotiable instruments, it would be disastrous to undertake the legislative enactment of the law of corporations. The gradual invasion of common law by statute has long been in progress with no serious difficulties. A wholly different situation would be created by the codification at a single stroke of the entire common law and the transfer from the courts to the legislature of the future development of the law.

In all legal systems the development of the law has depended not upon the legislature or the courts but upon the wisdom and skill of the men who occupied official positions. Wise men have recognized that all law is at bottom case law. In other words, the rules of law spring not from the fertile imagination of jurists and legislators but from the necessities of everyday life. In some countries the statement of the rules will best proceed from the judges, and in other countries this will be left to the legislators. But from whatever source derived, the rules will be sound only if they are in accord with the situations to which they apply.

Part Two

FORMS AND METHODS
OF TRIAL

VIII

The Older Modes of Trial

COMPURGATION, OR WAGER OF LAW

COMPURGATION, OR WAGER OF LAW, came into the English legal system long after it had made its appearance on the continent of Europe.[1] The origin of compurgation is said to be connected with the solidarity of the family group. Since the oath that was spoken was in the nature of a character assertion, it was appropriate that it should be given by those who best knew the accused. These were certainly his kinsmen, but in some communities kinsmen were expressly excluded from testifying in behalf of the accused. No definite conclusions, therefore, can be reached that compurgation was an outgrowth of family relationships.

The number of compurgators was not everywhere the same, although only one task was required of them. They swore not to the truth or falsity of the facts in the case but only to the credibility of the oath given by the accused. After the defendant had made

[1] There has been little written on compurgation, except in connection with other older forms of trial. H. C. Lea, *Superstition and Force*, 4th ed. (Philadelphia, 1892), Part I, is the best summary in English. See also J. B. Thayer, *Preliminary Treatise on Evidence* (Boston, 1898), Ch. I.

oath denying the charge, "likewise, witnesses of his own order, who were eyewitnesses and cognizant of the facts in the case, swore after him that the aforesaid N. had given a true and satisfactory oath in what he had sworn regarding the matter."[2] Actually the compurgators, or oath helpers, did not have to know the facts of the matter in litigation; their testimony was confined to the credibility of the oath given by their principal.

The character of the accused had bearing on the number of compurgators. A known scoundrel would have difficulty in procuring any witnesses to the truth of his oath. On the other hand, a man who was prominent in the community and widely respected would have no trouble to bring into court an almost unlimited number of compurgators. The number of oath helpers most frequently found in the records is thirty-six, although many other figures are given at different times and places. In its most ancient form the Salic law required twenty-five compurgators to be chosen equally by both parties.

The plaintiff as a rule took oath that his claim was valid, and this did not always require corroboration. The burden of proof was on the defendant, and the number of compurgators that might be required of him depended upon his rank and the gravity of the case. In general it may be said that the more serious the offense the greater must be the number of compurgators. Among the Anglo-Saxons, the value of a man's oath was rated according to his rank. Since the compurgators had to be of the same rank as their principal, it necessarily followed that the lower the rank of the accused the more compurgators were required.

The method of selecting compurgators was also important in determining the result. Originally these were chosen by the accused, who gathered them from among his relatives and friends. This would lead almost inevitably to his acquittal. Other methods of selection had, therefore, to be devised. Perhaps the most rational of these was the one promulgated by Canute, who directed that

[2] *Translations and Reprints* (Department of History, University of Pennsylvania), IV, p. 3.

fourteen names be submitted to the defendant among whom he was required to find eleven willing to take the oath with him. It is probable that the selection was made by the sheriff and that challenges for competent cause were permitted.

The central feature of compurgation is, of course, the oath. Among Christians, the oath has attained great significance. This is somewhat difficult to understand because Christ taught that his followers should always speak the truth, and whatever goes beyond the simple statement of the truth "cometh of evil." It would therefore appear redundant to require a Christian to declare that what he said was the whole truth and nothing but the truth. Furthermore, it might seem almost offensive to the Christian to be required to state that his evidence is given under an immediate sense of his responsibility to God. The addition of the oath to the testimony of a Christian implies some doubt as to the strength of his religious convictions.

But the oath is much older than the Christian religion. It is found in all stages of society from barbarians to highly civilized states. Perhaps the most solemn oaths are those recorded in the Old Testament. In any case, modern uses of the oath require that it be administered to persons regardless of their religious beliefs. The oath has become a device to insure against perjury, or at least to enable perjury to be readily detected and subjected to punishment.

Although compurgation was almost universal among the countries of western Europe, confidence in the institution was somewhat qualified. The primitive law of the Frisians made the penalty for false swearing very severe.

He who seeks the composition for homicide, let him swear on the relics of the saints that he will not accuse any one of this except those whom he suspects of the murder; and then let him accuse of homicide one, two, or even three or four or however many there may have been that wounded him who was killed. But, though there were twenty or thirty, yet no more than seven can be accused, and let each one of these who has been accused swear with his twelfth hand [that is, with eleven compurgators], and after the oath let him show himself innocent by the judgment of God in the ordeal of boiling water. Let the one who swore first go first to the ordeal, and so on in order. He who shall be found guilty by the ordeal, let him pay the composition for homicide, and to the king double his *wergild;* let the others who were his oath helpers pay the fine for perjury as has previously been enacted.[3]

The penalty for perjury varied in the different codes, but was usually the loss of a hand.

In some codes a distinction was made between false swearing by compurgators and by witnesses. The theory was that a witness could not perjure himself unintentionally, he must have knowledge of the facts to which he swore. On the other hand, compurgators might not always know the facts and were therefore entitled to the benefit of the doubt. If they had not knowingly indulged in false swearing they were entitled to the privilege of redeeming their hands.

In many jurisdictions, a man nominated as a compurgator could not decline to serve without incurring a penalty. In the Lombard law, a man who declined this service had to swear that he dared not take the oath for fear of his soul. The statutes of Nieuport in 1163 provided a heavy penalty, and in addition pronounced condemnation, when any one of the compurgators declined the oath. Obviously a failure in the compurgation led to conviction or condemnation.

Compurgation, although amply rooted in the traditions of European peoples, was strongly opposed by civil authorities almost everywhere. Nevertheless, popular confidence was generally not lacking, and it was not until the Church undertook to check the abuses to which compurgation led, that the decline of the institution can be seen. About 1130 the Pope ordered that the oath of the compurgators should be simply as to their belief in the oath of the principal. Innocent III shortly thereafter directed that "those who are brought forward to purge another of infamy are held to affirm this alone by their oaths; namely, that they believe that he who is being purged speaks the truth."[4] Thus compurgators no longer

[3] *Ibid.,* p. 6.   [4] *Ibid.,* p. 7.

shared the guilt or innocence of the accused. Compurgation therefore lost the confidence of the people at the same time that it ceased to be of value in a court of justice.

There is another and perhaps more important reason for the decline of compurgation than the removal of church support. This is to be found in the revival of the study and application of the Roman law. As the work of the Roman jurists penetrated legal systems in southern Europe, compurgation lingered only in northern countries. Although compurgation was not abolished by statute in England until 1833, it had long been supplanted in practice by other forms of trial.

Reliance upon appeals to the supernatural has been so common in nearly all systems of law that it is not surprising that remnants of the practice remain in modern times. Insistence upon oath-taking has been relaxed only in favor of the members of some religious groups, such as the Society of Friends, who are permitted to affirm instead of swear to the truth of their testimony. Some people may be awed by the formality of an oath taken in the sight of God, whereas others regard this as a part of the routine of court procedure. In any case, the taking of an oath is today no deterrent to false swearing. It is only when a person is mindful of the penalties for perjury that he will be cautious in giving testimony. There is no longer any efficacy in the appeal to the supernatural.

THE ORDEAL

The ordeal is one of the oldest forms of trial.[5] It has been used by almost all peoples at some stage of their development. Among primitive peoples, its influence has been widespread and profound. The savage pack, it is true, did not know the ordeal, but the institu-

[5] There are some excellent accounts of the ordeal. The best single work in English is H. C. Lea, *Superstition and Force*, 4th ed. rev. (Philadelphia 1892), Part III. A very full treatment of the judgment of God, with citations from authorities, will be found in F. Patetta, *Le Ordalie* (Turin, 1884). The relation of the ordeal to law is discussed by H. Goitein, *Primitive Ordeal and Modern Law* (London, 1923).

tion made its appearance as soon as the agricultural stage of society was reached. The appeal to the supernatural, which is the essential feature of the ordeal, presupposes that the primitive human hordes have already formed social groups and have attained a belief in superior deities who watch over the common interests and dispense justice.

Whatever may have been the circumstances attending the use of the ordeal elsewhere, among the barbarians who settled in the Roman provinces it is likely that the custom of allowing each race to retain its own system of law explains the general recourse to the ordeal. The confusion which resulted when two or more litigants of different racial groups appeared in court made it almost impossible to rely upon human testimony. An appeal to the judgment of God became the only practicable form of procedure.

The ordeal as it appeared in judicial procedure in western Europe, except the ordeal of the cross, involved generally the exposure of the accused to fire or water. The water might be cold or hot, and the fire might be in the form of red-hot iron which the accused carried or walked upon or it might be a mass of flames through which he was obliged to pass. In any case, nobody doubted that the outcome was determined by God. The burden of proof was upon the accused, who with the help of God would pass through the ordeal unscathed. If he could not do this, he must be adjudged guilty of the charge lodged against him. There could be no compromise. The disputant was either entirely right or absolutely wrong. The purpose of the ordeal, then, was simply to distinguish between right and wrong.

In the conduct of the ordeal, participation by the Church was necessary. Without the intervention of the clergy, the ordeal could not be regarded as an undoubted appeal to God. The Church not only acquired vast influence in the administration of justice but also derived large revenues from the fees charged for the services of the priests. The local churches found in the ordeal a source of power and profit which led the parish priests to oppose papal efforts to abolish the institution. Gradually, however, the papacy won in the struggle with the local clergy to abolish the ordeal. The Fourth Lateran Council in 1215 forbade the employment of any ecclesiastical ceremonies in connection with the ordeal. This was a serious blow to its continued existence, because the moral influence of the ordeal depended entirely upon its religious associations. When the Decretals of Gregory IX were issued in 1234, the prohibitions previously directed to the clergy to abstain from assisting in the ordeal were broadened to a general condemnation of the entire system.

The ordeal of cold water was of great antiquity, having been mentioned in the books of ancient India, but it is doubtful whether it was used in Europe much before the ninth century. The basis of this ordeal was the belief that the pure water would not receive a person guilty of crime. In other words, the innocent would sink and the guilty float when thrown upon the water. Hincmar of Rheims in the ninth century described the cold water ordeal as follows:

Now the one about to be examined is bound by a rope and cast into the water because, as it is written, each one shall be holden with the cords of his iniquity. And it is evident that he is bound for two reasons; to wit, that he may not be able to practice any fraud in connection with the judgment, and that he may be drawn out at the right time if the water should receive him as innocent, so that he perish not. For as we read that Lazarus, who had been dead four days (by whom is signified each one buried under a load of crimes), was buried wrapped in bandages and, bound by the same bands, came forth from the sepulchre at the word of the Lord and was loosed by the disciples at his command; so he who is to be examined by this judgment is cast into the water bound, and is drawn forth again bound, and is either immediately set free by the judgment of the judges, being purged, or remains bound till the time of his purgation and is then examined by the court. . . . And in this ordeal of cold water whoever, after the invocation of God, Who is the Truth, seeks to hide the truth by a lie, cannot be submerged in the waters above which the voice of the Lord God has thundered; for the pure nature of the water recognizes as impure and therefore rejects as inconsistent with itself such human nature as has once been regenerated by the waters of baptism and is again infected by false-hood.[6]

Whatever may have been the reasons for the introduction of the cold water ordeal in medieval Europe, its use was early prohibited by imperial decree. Both Louis le Débonnaire and his son the Emperor Lothair spoke against it. The prohibitions proved ineffective, perhaps because they were not confirmed by the canons of authoritative councils. The cold water ordeal, supported by popular superstition, spread rapidly throughout Europe. Although it disappeared in time from criminal procedure, this form of ordeal was long retained in cases of sorcery and witchcraft. Trials for witchcraft lingered in some parts of Europe until the nineteenth century, although the cold water ordeal was no longer recognized in authorized legal procedures.

The ordeal of boiling water came to Europe from the East and is undoubtedly of great antiquity. No other mode of trial is mentioned in the Lex Salica. It was a favorite with both ecclesiastical and secular authorities and was attended with elaborate ceremonies. From the breviary of Eberhard of Bamburg in the late Middle Ages, the following formula for the conduct of the ordeal of boiling water is taken:

Let the priest go to the church with the prosecutors and with him who is about to be tried. And while the rest wait in the vestibule of the church let the priest enter and put on the sacred garments except the chasuble and, taking the Gospel and the chrismarium and the relics of the saints and the chalice, let him go to the altar and speak thus to all the people standing near: Behold, brethren, the offices of the Christian religion. Behold the law in which is hope and remission of sins, the holy oil of the chrisma, the consecration of the body and blood of our Lord. Look that ye be not deprived of the heritage of such great blessing and of participation in it by implicating yourselves in the crime of another, for it is written, not only are they worthy of death who do these things but they that have pleasure in them that do them.

Then let him thus address the one who is to undertake the ordeal:

[6] *Translations and Reprints,* IV, No. 4 (Department of History, University of Pennsylvania, 1898), pp. 11–12.

I command thee, N., in the presence of all, by the Father, the Son, and the Holy Ghost, by the tremendous day of judgment, by the ministry of baptism, by thy veneration for the saints, that, if thou art guilty of this matter charged against thee, if thou hast done it, or consented to it, or hast knowingly seen the perpetrators of this crime, thou enter not into the church nor mingle in the company of Christians unless thou wilt confess and admit thy guilt before thou art examined in public judgment.

Then he shall designate a spot in the vestibule where the fire is to be made for the water, and shall first sprinkle the place with holy water, and shall also sprinkle the kettle when it is ready to be hung and the water in it, to guard against the illusions of the devil. Then, entering the church with the others, he shall celebrate the ordeal mass. After the celebration let the priest go with the people to the place of the ordeal, the Gospel in his left hand, the cross, censer, and relics of the saints being carried ahead, and let him chant seven penitential psalms with a litany.

Prayer over the boiling water: O God, just Judge, firm and patient. who art the Author of peace, and judgest truly, determines what is right, O Lord, and make known Thy righteous judgment. O Omnipotent God, Thou that lookest upon the earth and makest it to tremble, Thou that by the gift of Thy Son, our Lord Jesus Christ, didst save the world and by His most holy passion didst redeem the human race, sanctify, O Lord, this water being heated by fire. Thou that didst save the three youths, Sidrac, Misac, and Abednego, cast into the fiery furnace at the command of Nebuchadnezzar, and didst lead them forth unharmed by the hand of Thy angel, do Thou O clement and most holy Ruler, give aid if he shall plunge his hand into the boiling water, being innocent, and, as Thou didst liberate the three youths from the fiery furnace and didst free Susanna from the false charge, so, O Lord, bring forth his hand safe and unharmed from this water. But if he be guilty and presume to plunge in his hand, the devil hardening his heart, let Thy holy justice deign to declare it, that Thy virtue may be manifest in his body and his soul be saved by penitence and confession. And if the guilty man shall try to hide his sins by the use of herbs or any magic, let Thy right hand deign to bring it to no account. Through Thy only begotten Son, our Lord Jesus Christ, who dwelleth with Thee.

Benediction of the water: I bless thee, O creature of water, boiling above the fire, in the name of the Father, and of the Son, and of the Holy Ghost, from whom all things proceed; I adjure thee by Him who ordered thee to water the whole earth from the four rivers, and who summoned thee forth from the rock, and who changed thee into wine, that no wiles of the devil or magic of men be able to separate thee from thy virtues as a medium of judgment; mayest thou punish the vile and the wicked, and purify the innocent. Through Him whom hidden things do not escape and who sent thee in the flood over the whole earth to destroy the wicked and who will yet come to judge the quick and the dead and the world by fire. Amen.

Prayer: Omnipotent, Eternal God, we humbly beseech Thee in behalf of this investigation which we are about to undertake here amongst us that iniquity may not overcome justice but that falsehood may be subjected to truth. And if anyone seek to hinder or obscure this examination by any magic or by herbs of the earth, deign to bring it to naught by Thy right hand, O upright Judge.

Then let the man who is to be tried, as well as the kettle or pot in which is the boiling water, be fumed with the incense of myrrh, and let this prayer be spoken: O God, Thou who within this substance of water hast hidden Thy most solemn sacraments, be graciously present with us who invoke Thee, and upon this element made ready by much purification pour down the virtue of Thy benediction that this creature, obedient to Thy mysteries, may be endued with Thy grace to detect diabolical and human fallacies, to confute their inventions and arguments, and to overcome their multiform arts. May all the wiles of the hidden enemy be brought to naught that we may clearly perceive the truth regarding those things which we with finite senses and simple hearts are seeking from Thy judgment through invocation of Thy holy name. Let not the innocent, we beseech Thee, be unjustly condemned, or the guilty be able to delude with safety those who seek the truth from Thee, who art the true Light, who seest in the shadowy darkness, and who makest our darkness light. O Thou who perceivest hidden things and knowest what is secret, show and declare this by Thy grace and make the knowledge of the truth manifest to us who believe in Thee.

Then let the hand that is to be placed in the water be washed with soap and let it be carefully examined whether it is sound; and before it is thrust in let the priest say: I adjure thee, O vessel, by the Father, and the Son, and the Holy Ghost, and by the holy resurrection, and by the tremendous day of judgment, and by the four Evangelists that if this man be guilty of this crime either by deed or by consent, let the water boil violently, and do thou, O vessel, turn and swing.

After this let the man who is to be tried plunge in his hand, and afterwards let it be immediately sealed up. After the ordeal let him take a drink of holy water. Up to the time of the decision regarding the ordeal it is a good thing to mix salt and holy water with all his food and drink.[7]

This formula is not different from that used elsewhere and in other times within the Christian era for the ordeal of boiling water. The elements of fire and water were combined, and the representation of the flood which had overcome the world in the time of Noah was joined with the fiery doom of the future which many believed would in the day of judgment overtake the earth. The extent to which the clergy could participate in this ordeal was almost unlimited and thereby they might enrich their parish treasuries enormously. Sometimes the extent of exposure to the boiling water was regulated, the depth of the hand sufficing for lesser charges whereas for more serious offenses the accused was required to plunge his arm to the elbow in the vessel. In all its variations the ordeal of boiling water was regarded as an ideal appeal to the judgment of God.

More popular in the Middle Ages than the ordeal of boiling water was the ordeal by fire applied directly or indirectly to the person of the accused. The ordeal of red-hot iron was introduced throughout the whole of Europe. In the code of the Frankish kingdoms of the East it is the only form mentioned, except the duel, and it there retained its legal authority long after it had become obsolete elsewhere. The method of conducting an ordeal of red-hot iron is described in a tenth century doom of King Aethelstan as follows:

If anyone shall have given pledge to undergo the ordeal of iron . . . , let him go three days beforehand to the priest whose duty it is to bless him with the sign of the cross; and let him live upon bread, water, salt, and herbs, and hear mass each one of the three days; and let him make his offering and go to the holy communion on the day when he is to be examined by the ordeal; and before he is examined let him swear that by the law of the realm he is innocent of the charge. . . . Concerning the ordeal we enjoin in the name of God and by the command of the archbishop and of all our bishops that no one enter the church after the fire has been brought in with which the ordeal is to be heated except the

[7] *Ibid.*, pp. 7–10.

priest and him who is to undergo judgment. And let nine feet be measured off from the stake to the mark, by the feet of him who is to be tried. . . . . And when the ordeal is ready let two men from each side go in and certify that it is as hot as we have directed it to be. Then let an equal number from both sides enter and stand on either side of the judgment place along the church, and let them all be fasting and abstinent from their wives on the preceding night. And let the priest sprinkle them all with water and let them bow themselves everyone to the holy water and let the holy Gospel and the cross be given them all to kiss. And no one shall mend the fire any longer than the beginning of the hallowing, but let the iron lie on the coals until the last collect. Afterwards let it be placed on a frame, and let no one speak except to pray diligently to God, the Father Omnipotent, to deign to manifest His truth in the matter. And let the accused drink of the holy water and then let the hand with which he is about to carry the iron be sprinkled, and so let him go [to the ordeal]. Let the nine feet that were measured off be divided into three sections. In the first division let him hold his right foot, close to the stake. Then let him move his right foot across the second into the third division, where he shall cast the iron in front of him and hasten to the holy altar. Then let his hand be sealed up, and on the third day let examination be made whether it is clean or foul within the wrapper. And whoever shall transgress these laws, be the ordeal of no worth in his case, but let him pay the king a fine of twenty shillings.[8]

Sometimes the ordeal of red-hot iron involved the placing of glowing ploughshares on the pavement of the church upon which the accused was required to walk. The story is told that Edward the Confessor required his mother Queen Emma to undertake the ordeal of burning shares when she was accused of criminal intimacy with Alwyn, Bishop of Winchester. According to the account, which was written at a much later time, the queen supported by two bishops walked upon the shares barefooted and unharmed.[9]

The ordeal by fire, administered directly, without the intervention either of water or of iron, was prescribed in the code of the Ripuarian Franks to be used in cases of slaves or foreigners. But there is no doubt that the ordeal of fire in a number of forms was

---

[8] *Ibid.*, pp. 12–13.   [9] *Ibid.*, pp. 13–14.

used in many parts of Europe. The ceremonies attending this ordeal were carefully regulated by the priests, and the size and substance of the wood to be burned were closely prescribed. In one such ordeal "the fire was made of dry olive branches, covering a space thirteen feet long; and there were two piles with a space about a foot wide between them. The height of these piles was four feet."[10] The record shows that the ordeal by fire was frequently claimed by ecclesiastics. This may have been done in order to make a profound impression on the spectators. On the other hand, it has been suggested that the priests, in whose hands the arrangement of all the details was placed, could in most instances manage to secure the desired results.

Although the ordeals by fire and water were the chief forms assumed by the institution, a number of less popular ordeals existed at different times. Perhaps the most important of these was the ordeal of the cross. This was a simple test of endurance and was undergone by both parties to a dispute. In the ordeal of the cross, the two litigants were placed standing before a crucifix with their arms outstretched; the one who was able to maintain this position the longer won his case. A capitulary of Charlemagne directed that this form of ordeal be used in territorial disputes. The capitulary provides:

If a dispute, contention, or controversy shall arise between the parties regarding the boundaries or limits of their kingdoms of such a nature that it cannot be settled or terminated by human evidence, then we desire that for the decision of the matter the will of God and the truth of the dispute may be sought by means of the judgment of the cross, nor shall any sort of battle or duel ever be adjudged for the decision of any such question.

The ordeal of the cross received early condemnation by the secular authorities. A capitulary of Louis le Débonnaire forbade anyone to undertake any sort of ordeal of the cross, "lest that which was glorified by the passion of Christ should be brought into contempt through anyone's temerity."[11]

[10] *Ibid.*, p. 14.   [11] *Ibid.*, p. 16.

The unsparing condemnation of the ordeal by the papacy, which culminated in the prohibitions of the Fourth Lateran Council in 1215, was seconded by the secular authorities. Henry III in his instructions to the royal judges on circuit throughout England in 1219 directed that other modes of proof be employed, "inasmuch as the Roman Church has prohibited the judgment of fire and water." By the middle of the thirteenth century only the wager of battle appears to have been retained in the judicial procedure of England, the ordeals of fire and water having been abandoned. The Emperor Frederic II in 1231 pronounced against the ordeal at the same time subjecting it to ridicule. "Indeed," he said, "we consider that they deserve ridicule rather than instruction who have so little understanding as to believe that the natural heat of red-hot iron grows mild, nay, (what is more foolish) even turns to coldness without the working of an adequate cause; or who assert that on account of a troubled conscience alone a criminal does not sink into the cold water, when rather it is the holding in of sufficient air that does not allow of his being submerged."[12]

The disappearance of the ordeal cannot be attributed wholly to papal opposition. The growth of the law inevitably meant the displacement of the ordeal by other and more rational modes of trial. The ordeal is an appeal to influences which sway the individual because of their hold on his emotional nature. A mature system of law always involves an appeal to reason. In its development, there is reflected the gradual progress of the rational factors of the human mind. The decline of the ordeal coincided with the rise of the inquest which is essentially a rational form of procedure.

THE WAGER OF BATTLE

The wager of battle supplemented the ordeal, which it long survived. It is sometimes called an ordeal, "a God's judgment," but it has other aspects than that of an appeal to Heaven. There is in the

12 *Ibid.*, p. 18.

wager of battle an attempt to reduce to orderly procedure what might otherwise be an exercise of self help. Although unknown to the Greeks and the people of the Orient, the wager of battle was common throughout Central Europe and Scandinavia.[13] It originally sprang from the belief that through interposition of the deity victory would be assured the more worthy of two contending parties. While the institution is entirely out of harmony with modern conceptions of justice, the practice of submitting disputes to the chances of an equal combat, and there were early efforts towards equalization of the opposing parties, was certainly an advance over the more primitive blood feud.

Wager of battle should be distinguished from the private duel. There are conflicting views regarding the origin of the private duel, but the generally accepted view is that the duel of honor arose in feudal Europe during the age of chivalry and after the decline of the judicial combat. The distinction between the two institutions is mainly one of objective. The judicial combat was intended to be a means of determining the truth in doubtful cases of dispute, while the private duel aimed to provide reparation or atonement for wounded honor.

Although the wager of battle existed among all the Teutonic peoples of western Europe, it does not appear to have been brought to England by the Anglo-Saxons. It was not until after the Norman Conquest that the wager of battle became a part of English judicial procedure. By that time it had disappeared in Italy, Spain, and southern France, where the influence of Roman law and institutions was strongly in opposition to the procedure. The later Middle

[13] The literature on the wager of battle is not extensive. An excellent account is given in *Superstition and Force*, Part II; a briefer statement is given in F. A. Inderwick, *The King's Peace* (London, 1895), pp. 62–68. The most complete account of the judicial duel in England and Scotland is to be found in George Neilson, *Trial by Combat* (Glasgow, 1890). Earlier accounts are to be found in J. Selden, *The Duello, or Single Combat* (London, 1610); T. Madox, *History of the Exchequer* (London, 1769), Vol. I, and W. Dugdale, *Origines Judiciales* (London, 1761). Typical appeals are set forth in *Select Pleas of the Crown* (Selden Society Publications, ed. F. W. Maitland, Vol. I, London, 1888).

Ages found the wager of battle only in the northern countries of Europe.

Banished by the people of Iceland in 1011 and by the Danes in 1074, trial by battle became chiefly associated with northern France. It was at first hateful to the people of England. In the so-called "Laws of William the Conqueror," it figures as being the Frenchman's mode of trial and not the Englishman's. In a generation after the Conquest, the charter of Henry I to the city of London granted exemption from it; and the same exemption was elsewhere widely sought and given. Its use was strongly resisted by competitive forms of procedure, the ordeal and compurgation. Despite this opposition, wager of battle survived in England, and evidences of its use are to be found down to the nineteenth century.

The wager of battle was available in both criminal and civil suits. Reproduced as a frontispiece to Professor Maitland's *Select Pleas of the Crown*, published by the Selden Society, is a picture taken from an Assize of the time of Henry III which represents a judicial combat between Walter Bloweberme and Hamo le Stare. Walter was an approver, or a criminal who had confessed his crime and received a pardon conditional on his accusing and vanquishing a certain number of his associates. Hamo was one of those accused by Walter of complicity in a robbery and defeated by him. The ultimate fate of Hamo is depicted on the gallows in the background.

The record which accompanies the picture is as follows:

The same Walter [Bloweberme] comes and appeals Hamo le Stare of Winchester by the same words [as he has used in his other appeals] to wit that they were . . . the Cross at Winchester, and there stole certain clothes and other goods, whereof Hamo had as his share two coats, to wit, one of Irish cloth and another coat half of Abingdon cloth and half of London Burrell [a kind of coarse cloth]; and that he (Hamo) was along with him [Walter] in committing the said larcency, he [Walter] offers to deraign against him [Hamo] as the court shall consider. And Hamo comes and defends all of it [and says] that he will battle between them. And the battle between them is struck. And the said Hamo has been defeated. Therefore to judgment against him, etc. He had no chattels.[14]

Civil causes for which trial by battle was undertaken dealt chiefly with claims to lands. These seldom arose in England after the twelfth century. The procedure at that time became limited almost exclusively to criminal cases, especially the "appeal of murder" or the right of the nearest of kin to wage battle with the accused when acquitted on a public indictment. This assumed the form of a privilege which was successfully defended in Parliament in 1774 when that body agreed to pass a bill relating to the Massachusetts Bay Colony only after the ministers had struck out a clause denying the colonists the appeal of murder. It was not until 1819 that this privilege was formally abolished. In 1818 the celebrated case of Ashford v. Thornton had arisen. On the public indictment accusing Thornton of murdering Ashford's sister, the accused was acquitted despite strong evidence of his guilt. Popular feeling was aroused, and the brother of the dead girl, aided by a public subscription, instituted an appeal of murder to try the case again. This procedure, although unusual, was competent, and the prisoner appeared before Lord Ellenborough and three other judges. When asked to plead, he declared that he was not guilty and that he was ready to defend his plea with his body. "Then he threw down a gauntlet without either fingers or thumbs, made of white tanned skin, ornamented with sewn tracery and silk fringes, crossed by a narrow band of red leather, with leathern tags and thongs for fastening." The judges were greatly averse to granting the duel, but the attorneys of Thornton had carefully prepared their case, and Lord Ellenborough was obliged to declare that it was the law of the land. However, Ashford had no desire to engage in a duel, so the appeal was withdrawn and Thornton was set free. The following year Parliament passed the Appeal of Murder Act, and the last vestige of the wager of battle disappeared in England.

The procedure in the duel or actual combat which Ashford declined was in the Middle Ages carefully defined. The parties met

[14] *Select Pleas of the Crown*, p. xxix.

at the appointed time and place before the judge. The accused first took oath, with his right hand on a Bible held by a priest and with his left hand grasping the accuser's right hand, that he was innocent. The accuser in like manner swore that the accused was guilty. The two parties were then led into the lists, the accused taking his position on the east side facing his opponent on the west side. At this point the contestants took a second oath declaring that they had not employed magic to aid in the fight. A court officer proclaimed loudly that no one was to speak or move during the battle. Arms were then given to the combatants, prayers were recited and a benediction was pronounced by the priest, and the duel was begun. Generally, the battle lasted until the death of one combatant or his admission of defeat, although in some cases it might terminate by a confession of guilt and the payment of a fine by the accused. The struggle might last an entire day, but if the accuser was not victor by nightfall he lost his cause. Defeat for the accuser meant that he must forever wear the calfskin, a sign of dishonor, while the punishment for the unsuccessful accused, if not already slain, was death by hanging.

The use of champions in judicial combat affords an interesting development in the history of the procedure. Originally champions were permitted in cases where one or both parties were under disability because of age or physical infirmity. Women were regularly allowed to enter the duel through the representation of champions. At first, the champions were the next of kin or close relatives of the contending parties. Later, able-bodied antagonists put forward substitutes, whether connected with them or not by ties of blood, who fought the battle for their principals.

The practice of hiring champions to fight a judicial duel brought the institution into disrepute.

Reckless desperadoes, skilled at quarter-staff, or those whose familiarity with sword and dagger, gained by a life spent in ceaseless brawls, gave them confidence in their own ability, might undertake it as an occupation which exposed them to little risk beyond what they habitually incurred, and of such was the profession generally composed.

This evil must have made itself apparent early, for we find Charlemagne endeavoring to oppose it by decreeing that no robber should be allowed to appear in the lists as a champion, and the order needed to be frequently repeated.[15]

Throughout much of continental Europe the occupation of champion became infamous while in England prolonged efforts were put forth to suppress their hiring.

Ecclesiastical opposition to the wager of battle culminated in 1215 in the prohibitions of the Fourth Lateran Council. It is, however, doubtful whether opposition to the procedure would have succeeded without the recovery of Roman law. Wager of battle had become one of the institutions of feudalism against which the Roman law provided a rational substitute the superiority of which could not be denied. The Christian Church had for centuries protested against trial by battle on religious grounds. Ecclesiastical penalties the Church could invoke, but over the secular courts there was only the power of persuasion. It was not until monarchs fell under the enchantment of the Roman law that the judicial duel, along with many other feudal institutions, began to disappear.

The countries of southern Europe, where the Roman law flourished almost continuously, were the first to decree the abolition of trial by battle. In 1231 the Emperor Frederic II in his Neapolitan code pronounced against the procedure, denying it to be a form of legal proof but a kind of divination contrary to every notion of justice and equity. Shortly thereafter the laws of Aragon prohibited judicial combat in both civil and criminal cases while Alfonso the Wise of Castile in the code generally known as Las Siete Partidas subjected the procedure to very important limitations.

In France the legislation of St. Louis and his successor Philip the Fair was strongly opposed to the judicial combat. But the nobles were always restive under prohibitions what sought to destroy their feudal privileges and after the death of Philip the Fair re-

15 *Superstition and Force*, p. 186.

gained the right to challenge accusers to trial by battle in criminal cases. Nevertheless, the wager of battle steadily declined in France through the fourteenth and fifteenth centuries. The power to grant or withhold the wager of battle became practically a prerogative of the crown. By the middle of the sixteenth century judicial combat had ceased to exist in France, although no general law prohibiting it appears to have been enacted; the custom died a natural death.

The failure to repeal the wager of battle as a part of English judicial procedure until the nineteenth century does not mean that it was frequently used. On the contrary, the rapid growth of the jury system rendered all other forms of trial of little significance. That trial by battle remained a legal form in England was the result of inadvertence.

IX

The Jury System

THE INSTITUTION OF TRIAL by jury is now recognized to have been derived from the Norman inquest; it was unknown in England before the coming of William the Conqueror.[1] The origin of trial by jury must be sought not in ancient popular custom but in royal privilege. The vigorous royal power built up by the Frankish rulers included an institution, the inquest, for discovering the extent of the king's rights in the community, especially in fiscal matters. This required that the best and most trustworthy men in each community should assemble in the local court where they swore to the best of their knowledge and belief what lands and what rights

---

[1] The account of the origin of the jury by H. Brunner, *Die Entstehung der Schwurgerichte* (Berlin, 1872) is now generally accepted. Some of Brunner's conclusions have been challenged by E. Meyer, *Geschworengericht und Inquisitionsprozess* (Munich, 1916). Brunner's results form the basis of the treatment of the jury in Pollock and Maitland, *History of English Law*, 2 vol. (Cambridge, 1899), and in W. S. Holdsworth, *History of English Law*, Vol. II (Boston, 1922). See also J. B. Thayer, *Preliminary Treatise on Evidence at the Common Law* (Boston, 1898). Brunner's book has rendered obsolete the study of W. Forsyth, *History of Trial by Jury* (New York, 1875). An excellent account of the early Norman jury will be found in C. H. Haskins, *Norman Institutions* (Cambridge, Mass., 1918), Ch. VI.

should belong to the king in the district. In the beginning, the inquest was a form of administrative rather than judicial procedure, and although occasionally granted as a privilege to the Church in order to protect church lands, it continued to be the regular means whereby the Frankish kings evaded the technicalities and rigor of folk law in determining the rights of the crown. The extension of the inquest to judicial procedure in the ordinary courts of law was the later work of the Normans.

INTRODUCTION OF THE JURY INTO ENGLAND

Introduced into England from Normandy soon after the Conquest, the sworn inquest was a prerogative procedure of the crown as it had been on the continent. But in the twelfth century it was extended by the king to his subjects. In the assize *utrum* of 1164, Henry II decreed that a jury of twelve men should decide certain cases of conflict between the claims of the Church and those of the State. The establishment of trial by jury in civil cases was followed in 1166 by the Assize of Clarendon which provided for indictment by local juries of accusation but which retained the ordeal for the trial of the chief cases.

The introduction of the trial jury in criminal cases did not occur until a somewhat later date. Although the Assize of Clarendon had specified the ordeal as the mode of trial, it is clear that by the beginning of the thirteenth century the jury was being used in criminal cases whenever the accused asked for it. The judges at this time apparently formed the habit of asking the accused whether he would submit to a trial by the country. That is to say, he was asked to submit the question of his guilt or innocence to a second jury chosen from the neighbors present in the court. The submission was purely voluntary; a prisoner who refused to plead before such a tribunal could not be tried at all. He could, however, be subjected to the *peine forte et dure,* or judicial torture, in an attempt to make him plead.

The establishment of the grand jury is readily traced to the Assize of Clarendon, because that document prescribes "for the maintenance of peace and justice, that inquiry shall be made in every county and in every hundred by the twelve most lawful men of the hundred and by the four most lawful men of every vill, upon oath that they shall speak the truth, whether in their hundred or vill there may be any man who is accused or believed to be a robber, murderer, thief, or a receiver of robbers, murderers, or thieves since the King's accession." The accused when brought before the court was required to undergo the ordeal of water. In certain circumstances an alternative procedure by oath helpers was permitted. In the latter case, the accused, if he was "of bad renown and publicly and evilly reputed by the testimony of many lawful men," was obliged to quit the kingdom and never return without the king's permission.

The development of the trial jury in criminal cases cannot be precisely determined. There is evidence that when the presenting jury had been assembled and had done its work, the judges sometimes asked whether the accused was guilty of the crime for which he had been indicted. From the expressions of guilt or innocence by the presenting jurors the judges based their findings and gave their decisions. Glanvill, whose famous treatise was completed before 1190, shows clearly the extent to which trial by jury had become accepted in civil suits. From his pages, one can also discover that the jury was only beginning to penetrate the criminal law as a mode of trial.

Nevertheless, the recorded cases in the first half of the thirteenth century show that jury trials in criminal cases were steadily increasing if for no other reason than the decline of other modes of trial. The judicial duel was not available to many litigants, because of their age or some physical incapacity, and the ordeal suffered a crippling blow in the prohibitions of the Fourth Lateran Council. Of course, legislation could have been enacted to require the accused to submit to trial by jury. The fact that this was not done indicates the extent to which the new mode of trial was an innovation, contrary to accepted ideas. The judges therefore contented themselves with asking the accused to consent to trial by the country and stimulating him to acceptance of the procedure. The Statute of Westminster I in 1275 enacted that notorious felons who refused to put themselves on inquests for felonies for which they were charged should be subjected to judicial torture. The time had not yet arrived when the jury had become compulsory in all cases.

COMPOSITION OF THE JURY

The jury was representative of the community. Its object was either to present the suspicions of the countryside, or, in the case of the petit jury, to express its final opinion. The membership should therefore reflect the knowledge and wisdom of the men of the community. When Fortescue wrote in 1468, the jury had become a body of impartial men who came into court with an open mind. The jurors did not find their verdicts out of their own knowledge of the events, but heard the evidence presented by the parties or their counsel in open court. Witnesses were placed under oath and cross-examined in the presence of the judges, the parties, their counsel, and the jury. In other words, the jury by the time of Fortescue had attained its modern form.[2]

At the outset, knights were regularly chosen to comprise the grand jury whereas the petit jury was required to be composed of lawful and impartial men of the community. Since the members of the presenting jury were in the earliest years of the institution asked to advise the judges as to the guilt or innocence of the accused, it sometimes happened that the trial jury was composed of knights. As the jury system evolved, it soon became the practice to summon twelve men to serve on a jury and to demand from them a unanimous verdict. Selection had to be made from the neighborhood. The verdict was not that of twelve jurors but the

[2] J. Fortesque, *De Laudibus Legum Angliae*. Translated by F. Gregor. (Cincinnati, 1874).

verdict of the community. Hence, it necessarily followed that the jurors must agree in giving their verdict.

It is a commonplace to state that the jury is concerned only with questions of fact. Bracton wrote: "Truth is to be had from the juror, justice and judgment from the judge." In other words, a clear distinction was to be maintained between the law and the facts, and the business of the jury was with the latter.

Fortescue speaks of the jurors as witnesses. He does not mean that they actually saw the events which are the subject of the litigation, but they become witnesses through hearing the testimony and the arguments of counsel. Thus, Fortescue became convinced of the superiority of the English system over the systems of European countries founded upon Roman law, where two witnesses are enough.

Here no one's cause or right fails by the death or failure of witnesses. No unknown witnesses are produced here, no paid persons, paupers, strangers, untrustworthy, or those whose condition or hostility is unknown. These witnesses are neighbors, able to live out of their own property, of good name and unsullied reputation, not brought into court by a party, but chosen by an official who is a gentleman and indifferent, and required to come before the judge. These men know everything which witnesses can tell them; these are aware of the trustworthiness or untrustworthiness, and the reputation of the witnesses who are produced.[3]

There is here revealed in this early account of the jury the essential characteristic of the institution. At its inception, the jurors relied upon their own private knowledge aided by the testimony of witnesses brought into court by the parties to the action. In the course of time they came to rely wholly upon the evidence placed before them and examined in court by counsel. The punishment of jurors for an erroneous verdict, which in early times was most severe, could no longer be maintained. A man could not be charged with perjury when he was giving judgment on what he heard in court; he could only be said to have made an error in judgment in

3 *Ibid.*, Ch. 26.

reaching a wrong conclusion from testimony which was often conflicting. A method of revising erroneous verdicts had to be devised.

The severe remedy of attaint against false verdicts given by members of the jury was replaced by fines upon obstinate jurors. On the continent, wherever the jury was used, it was the custom to punish jurors who swore falsely. But the attaint not only punished the jurors but also secured the reversal of the previous verdict. Jurors in the time of Elizabeth who refused to find as directed by the courts were fined and imprisoned. Thus matters stood in 1670 when Bushel's case came before Vaughan, C. J., who gave the memorable opinion which soon ended the fining of jurors for their verdicts, and vindicated their character as judges of fact.

BUSHEL'S CASE

Edward Bushel was a member of the jury which in 1670 acquitted the Quakers Penn and Mead when indicted for having held an unlawful assembly. As the verdict was against the direction of the judge, each of the jurors was fined forty marks. Bushel refused to pay and was committed to custody. Upon a habeas corpus proceeding, Chief Justice Vaughan held that the ground of Bushel's commitment was insufficient, and set him at liberty.

The opinion in this case assumes that the jury will give its verdict not only upon the basis of evidence heard in court but also upon their own private knowledge. The judge knows only what is brought out in court, whereas the jurors, who are chosen from the community, may have ground to discredit all that is given in evidence in court. It is absurd that a judge should fine a jury for going against their evidence when he knows but part of it, "for the better and greater part of the evidence may be wholly unknown to him; and this may happen in most cases, and often doth. . . ."

Although Chief Justice Vaughan retained the ancient view that a jury may depend upon private knowledge, he gave a large place to their independence. Jurors are the judges of evidence, whereas the courts are judges of the law. An honest mistake by the jury in arriving at a verdict required some corrective procedure. Already the decisions of the judges on matters of law were subject to proceedings in error, and it could not be maintained that the verdicts of jurors were irreversible. As Chief Justice Vaughan had pointed out, both functions involved the exercise of judgment. It therefore followed naturally between 1670 and the time of Blackstone that "new trials are every day awarded" on the ground that "the verdict was given *without*, or *contrary to*, evidence." The true qualification for a juror had become exactly the reverse of what it had been in the formative period of the jury. In order to give an impartial verdict, he had to enter the jury box wholly uninformed on the issue he was to decide.[4]

The granting of a new trial in civil cases was more readily established than in the criminal law. In the latter, the courts had to consider the rights of the crown at the same time that they paid heed to the ancient maxim that a man should not twice be placed in jeopardy of life or limb for the same offense. The English practice since 1721 has been to allow no new trial where the defendant in a criminal prosecution has been acquitted. In the United States, after a conviction, new trials are generally allowed in all criminal cases. Where there has been an acquittal, new trials are not allowed.

JUDICIAL TORTURE

Throughout the formative period of trial by jury, judicial torture continued as a recognized and legal mode of investigation. Indeed, it was not abolished until 1772. Torture had its origin in the distant past and appeared in many legal systems at early stages. It arose in the countries of continental Europe before its use in England. Thirteenth century English records show that many persons who refused trial by jury were rigorously imprisoned, but there is no proof that they were tortured. Neither Glanvill nor Bracton wrote about judicial torture. But soon thereafter, we learn of

[4] E. Jenks, "According to the Evidence," *Cambridge Legal Essays*, pp. 191–201.

prisoners who refused to put themselves on the country "that their imprisonment is to be of the most rigorous kind; they are ironed, they lie on the ground in the prison's worst place, they have a little bread one day, a little water the next. A few years later we hear that the prisoner is to be laden with as much iron as he can bear, and thus in the course of time the hideous *peine forte et dure* was developed."[5]

Some writers have erroneously sought to derive the right to trial by jury from the 39th chapter of Magna Carta. This provision recites: "No freeman shall be arrested, or detained in prison, or deprived of his freehold, or outlawed, or banished, or in any way molested; and we will not set forth against him, unless by the lawful judgment of his peers and by the law of the land." The identification of judgment by peers and trial by jury was not made until a much later date. "The mistake," McKechnie writes, "probably owes its origin to a not unnatural tendency of later generations of lawyers to explain what was unfamiliar in the Great Charter by what was familiar in their own experience. They found nothing in their own day to correspond with the *judicium parium* of 1215...; they found nothing in Magna Carta ... to correspond with their own trial by jury: Therefore they identified the two, interpreting the present chapter as a general guarantee of the right to trial by jury."[6]

The *judicium parium*, or judgment by peers, existed when King John gave his assent to Magna Carta. This was a product of feudalism and was intended when it was declared in 1215 to be a part of English law to apply only in cases between the king and his subjects. "Although the barons at no time objected to having their ordinary lawsuits judged in the common law courts, they felt strongly that their great cases, especially those where the king was a party, and those that concerned their rights in general, should be

---

[5] Pollock and Maitland, II, pp. 651–2.

[6] W. S. McKechnie, *Magna Carta* (Glasgow, 1905), p. 456. See also C. H. McIlwain, "Due Process of Law in Magna Carta," *Columbia Law Review*, XIV, pp. 27–51.

judged by their peers."[7] Since the great peers by the middle of the thirteenth century were found in Parliament, it was this tribunal which King John was required to recognize as having jurisdiction. The barons would have rejected the verdict of "twelve good men" of their own locality. What they wanted was a judgment on the whole case, which must from the beginning to the conclusion be conducted before men who were their equals.

The respective functions of judge and jury in English law are well understood on both sides of the Atlantic. There is abundant literature on the subject, and no serious proposals have been brought forward for the abolition of the jury in criminal prosecutions. At the same time, there has been a marked decline, especially in England, in the use of jury trials in civil suits. Modifications in form have been made over the centuries in both England and the United States, but changes in substance in the jury system have not been attempted.[8]

CONTINENTAL USES OF THE JURY

The French Revolution introduced the modern jury system upon the continent of Europe. For at least fifty years before the uprising of 1789, French jurists and legal writers had contemplated with approval the English judicial procedure. The English law received constant favorable mention in the debates of the National Assembly and its institutions were widely adopted. In order to imitate the English, some excellent features of old French procedure had to be sacrificed.

The National Assembly received on March 29, 1790, the plan of Mr. Duport for the reorganization of the judicial system. At this time, the jury was accepted, but for criminal cases only. The jury for civil cases was not adopted, and has been almost wholly un-

[7] B. C. Keeney, *Judgment by Peers* (Cambridge, Mass., 1949), p. 110.

[8] Some interesting comments on the modern jury system will be found in F. L. Wellman, *Gentlemen of the Jury* (New York, 1924). See also A. T. Vanderbilt, "Judges and Jurors: Their Functions, Qualification and Selection," *Boston University Law Review*, XXXVI, pp. 1–76.

known on the continent. In M. Duport's plan, an officer to be known as the "director of the jury" was to make the preliminary investigation and prepare the case for presentation to a jury of eight members, called the jury of accusation, which corresponds to the English grand jury. Subsequently, the jury of accusation was expunged and nobody has asked for its reestablishment. The final death blow to the grand jury was administered by Napoleon, who excluded it from his code.

The Napoleonic code rejected the English principle of unanimity in reaching a verdict. Instead, it provided "that the decision of the jury should be reached for or against the accused by a majority, otherwise to be void. In case of a tie, the opinion favorable to the accused should prevail."[9] Napoleon has been charged with lacking sympathy with the jury system, but he recognized that it was popular and saw in the institution something which might be used to his advantage. During the Terror, lawfully constituted juries had been under the control of the dominant faction, with great resulting abuses. Nevertheless, succeeding years led to a restoration of confidence in the trial jury.

In 1832 the entire law regulating the administration of justice was codified anew, but few important changes in the jury system were made. Generally speaking, all qualified electors have continued to be eligible for jury duty. The code recited that "no one can fill the office of juryman . . . if he does not enjoy civic, civil, and family rights, or if he is in a state of incapacity. . . ." A later provision excluded "domestic servants or hired servants and those who cannot read and write in French."[10]

An oath was taken by all jurors and witnesses. The counsel for defense was put under oath "to employ only the truth in the defense of the accused." Penalties were provided for false swearing.

Changes made in 1832 included a provision that the verdict of a trial jury must be "by a majority of more than seven voices," and

[9] A. Esmein, *History of Continental Criminal Procedure*. tr. J. Simpson (Boston, 1913), p. 513.
[10] *Ibid.*, p. 559.

that "the verdict shall never be subject to any appeal." At a later date, French procedure returned to a simple majority as necessary to render a verdict. Subsequent alterations of the code have been in matters of detail; the fundamental principles remain as they were adopted at the time of the French Revolution.[11]

The jury system was extended to nearly all countries on the continent of Europe. It has never been accepted in Holland, and did not appear in Norway until 1890. The other Scandinavian countries have not followed the example of Norway, so the jury does not exist in Denmark or Sweden. A special exception is made in Sweden where jury trials exist involving the freedom of the press. Wherever the jury system has been introduced on the continent, it has followed, in the main, the French pattern. Differences in detail have not been the result of differences in principles.

The jury in some continental countries has recently been threatened by the revival of lay judges, who sit with professional colleagues in cases of major crimes. The institution of lay judges is very old, dating from the Middle Ages when the schöffen presided over the local courts. Some advantages have been claimed in behalf of lay judges, who bring to the court a somewhat broader view of the issues than their professional colleagues. At the same time, German experience has shown that judges trained in the law tend to overawe their lay associates.

There is a fundamental unity among continental countries in matters of criminal procedure. This is due largely to faithful adherence to the French model of the code of Napoleon. The public prosecutor is found almost everywhere on the continent and the initiation of prosecutions is almost wholly in his hands. The jury, with few exceptions, is composed of twelve qualified electors whose conduct is prescribed by law. In a few countries, one or two extra jurors are placed in the jurybox in order that there may be no mistrial in the event of illness or incapacity of a member of the jury. The verdict is rendered by a simple majority of the

[11] W. B. Scaife, "Some European Modifications of the Jury System," *American Historical Association Annual Report, 1894*, pp. 125–40.

jurors, although a two-thirds vote was required by the German code of criminal procedure of 1877. Although many changes of detail in the codes of criminal procedure, including the institution of the jury, have been made in the countries of continental Europe, almost no deviations have been made from long established principles.

Part Three

LAW IN THE MODERN WORLD

X

Roman Law in the Modern World

THE INFLUENCE OF ROMAN LAW in the modern world has not been exhausted by its contributions to systems of national law.[1] That is to say, the formation of civil codes, embodying large elements of Roman law in their construction, does not comprise the whole or even the main borrowing from Rome. The Codes Napoleon were copied outside France in the nineteenth century just as the writings of Bartolus and other commentators supplied the materials of the Corpus Juris, as recovered by the glossators, to the jurists of an earlier day. But this is not to tell the whole story. Much Roman

---

[1] The contributions of Roman law to the modern world have been described by a number of German writers since the time of Savigny. The recent work of Egon Weiss, *Institutionem des Römischen Privatrechts als Einführung in die Rechts-Ordnung der Gegenwart*, 2nd. ed. (Stuttgart, 1949), is excellent. In English there is the work of C. P. Sherman, *Roman Law in the Modern World*, 3 vol. 2nd ed. (New York, 1924) and J. Mackintosh, *Roman Law in Modern Practice* (Edinburgh, 1934). See also W. W. Buckland and A. D. McNair, *Roman Law and Common Law*, 2nd ed. (Cambridge, 1952) and the earlier work by T. E. Scrutton, *The Influence of the Roman Law on the Law of England* (Cambridge, 1885). A recent work by A. Berger, *Encyclopedic Dictionary of Roman Law* (Philadelphia, 1953) is of great value to students of comparative jurisprudence as well as specialists in the field of Roman law.

law is "secreted in the interstices of procedure," even in the common law system.

Any study of the influence of Roman law upon the subsequent legal development of continental Europe must begin in Italy. The whole of western Europe between the sixth and twelfth centuries witnessed the barbarization of Roman law to produce a kind of Romance law quite different from the classical law. In Italy alone, the Roman law, in its original form, never completely lost its hold. The scientific study of law as a part of the ancient culture never died out in Italy. Thus the traditions of Roman law continued not only among the learned jurists but also among the Italian people.

The jurists, however, were not particularly learned people, even for the time in which they lived. They lacked the intellectual power to embrace the whole of the Corpus Juris and contented themselves with the study of the Institutes and some of the Novels. They neglected almost entirely the Digest, which contains the living portion of the old Roman law. As a result, the jurists in their work following the reign of Justinian never succeeded in gaining any control over the practical administration of justice. Their greatest service was to keep alive the traditions of the original law. The rise of the glossators in the twelfth century restored the Corpus Juris of Justinian for the whole of western Europe.[2]

The achievements of the glossators have already been mentioned as well as the school of Commentators who followed them. Bartolus, his colleagues, and his pupils have been credited with adapting the *glossae* of the Bolognese scholars to the requirements of everyday court procedure. The great gloss of Accursius soon became a necessary accompaniment of legal study and practice in the courts of western European countries. By the seventeenth century it was possible to state as a rule, *quidquid non agnoscit glossa nec agnoscit curia*. That is to say, the unglossed parts of the Corpus Juris were not admitted into the courts of Italy or Germany.

It should not be overlooked that the medieval Church played an important role in bringing the Roman law into harmony with

[2] R. Sohm, *Institutes of Roman Law*. tr. Ledlie. 3rd ed. (Oxford, 1907), pp. 133-5.

the requirements of the age. As early as the eleventh century, the Pope at Rome became the unquestioned head of the Christian Church. Thenceforth, the Church gave law to its communicants upon a great variety of matters. This law was embodied first in the canons of the Church as compiled by Gratian and subsequently at the beginning of the fourteenth century in the *Corpus Juris Canonici.*

The canon law did not deal exclusively with ecclesiastical affairs, but sought to include private law, criminal law, and the law of procedure. These matters were dealt with on lines approved by the Church. Within the domain of private law there were no far-reaching reforms, but in the field of procedure and criminal law the changes were so extensive as to amount virtually to a revolution. Roman procedure and Roman criminal law were in fact transformed into the law of procedure and the criminal law of the canon law. But the canon law was accepted only in ecclesiastical courts; the secular courts received the Roman law at the hands of jurists who looked mainly to the glossators for guidance. Nevertheless, the Christian world had before it both kinds of law—canon and civil—from which it could fashion its legal institutions. The Church was never able to effect such a complete reform of Roman law as would enable it to dominate the secular courts.[3]

TRANSFORMATION OF THE OLDER ROMAN LAW

The tripartite division of the Roman law into the law of persons, things, and actions has been carried with modifications into modern legal systems. The law of persons as outlined by Gaius in the second century might today be said to deal with abnormal persons. Gaius analyzed the law of persons, classifying the rules as they applied to freemen and slaves, citizens and non-citizens, and dependence upon or independence of the power of the head of the household. The chief concerns of the law of persons are slavery, citizenship, and patria potestas.

[3] *Ibid.*, pp. 138–40.

The institution of slavery, which existed at Rome, has now disappeared from the civilized world. The rules of Roman law regulating the status of unfree persons have been dropped from modern systems of law. No one can alienate his liberty, and freedom is the natural and normal status of all persons.

Citizenship, which was an important factor in the early Roman law, lost much of its significance after A.D. 212, when the Emperor Caracalla made all free persons within the empire Roman citizens. The only exceptions in the edict were foreigners who were members of no political community. For all practical purposes there was only one class of citizens—free persons.

The citizenship of a person in Roman law and in modern systems is determined by domicile, that is, that place he has selected as his permanent residence. A Roman citizen might have several domiciles for purposes of business. Modern codes have permitted plurality of domiciles, but no one can have at one time more than one principal domicile. Modern law has merely repeated the Roman rule that a wife has the same domicile as her husband.

Family status was an important part of the law of persons at Rome. The rights and duties of a person were determined largely by the fact of his independence of, or dependence upon, paternal authority. The patriarchal theory of the family viewed the head of the household—father or grandfather—as the one member who sustained any legal relations to society or the state.

Modern law does not recognize paternal power to the extent found in Roman law. But many of the Roman rules regarding marriage and divorce are to be found in allotropic forms in the modern codes. What has disappeared from Roman family law in its passage through the centuries is the unlimited patria potestas. The head of a family continues to enjoy full control over his children, but this is terminated when the child becomes of full age or marries. As a matter of fact, the strict Roman rules attending family power had begun to be relaxed before the time of Justinian. The proprietary capacity of a son under parental authority was admitted during the period of the Roman republic if the son was in military service. A soldier might acquire for himself any property gained in war. This was later broadened to include property gained from anyone, except the paterfamilias, or head of the household. Parental rights over the property of descendants who had attained their majority were gradually abolished by statute or by imperial decree and have not reappeared in modern codes. It is only with respect to the property of minor children that parental rights resemble the rules of Roman law set forth by Justinian.

JURISTIC PERSONS

Artificial, or juristic persons, were also recognized in the Roman law. In the early records, the individual and the state were the only entities to which the law attached rights and duties. The early records of the Roman republic speak of Titius and the state. If a matter related to the state it was rigorously excluded from the domain of the private law and brought within the *jus publicum*, or public law. There were, it is true, societies, but none that enjoyed proprietary capacity. Property intended for the use of the society had to be formally vested in an individual member and treated as though it were his separate property.

The conception of a juristic person was not introduced into the private law of Rome until the time of the empire. The first Roman corporation to appear in the private law was the municipium. The development of a system of municipal government at the time of Augustus led to the inclusion within the rules of private law of the property of the municipality. The distinction was maintained between public and private corporations, the former being political bodies created to fulfill the purposes of government. Private corporations are organized either for some private purpose or for the welfare of the general public. But the property of a municipality which was indirectly beneficial to the individual members of the community, such as things used for the maintenance of schools or for the paving and lighting of streets, was brought within the private law. In this way the municipality became a person capable of private rights and duties.

The way was thus opened for the Romans to bring within the private law not only a great variety of charitable foundations and social and mutual benefit associations but also the many private corporations organized for the purposes of business, trade, and industry. The private corporation was definitely advantageous to imperial Rome. It enabled the patricians to invest money in business or mercantile pursuits without incurring the stigma of being personally engaged in trade. In early Roman law, no citizen could engage in trade without losing his political rights, and senators were forbidden by statute from engaging in any mercantile pursuit. Corporate enterprises were not less important to the plebeians and poorer people at Rome. These could become stockholders in a great corporation which enabled them to undertake large operations which would otherwise be possible only to the households of the patrician families with vast numbers of slaves. The corporation thus became a counterbalance in politics to the patrician household.

The legislation of Augustus provided that associations or corporations might be authorized if they could show an object helpful to the state or beneficial to the public. Soon the Roman law established as juristic persons all associations which were duly authorized, and the conception of an artificial person, previously applicable to public corporations, was extended to private associations, thus making them true private corporations. There never was a time within the empire when freedom of incorporation without state authorization was permitted. Modern law is the same as the Roman; the state alone can create a corporation.

Roman law required at least three persons to form a corporation. This number is commonly required by modern systems to form a corporation aggregate. The Roman corporation, once constituted, remained in existence regardless of membership changes. A corporation could still be maintained although reduced to a single member. This has led to the modern corporation sole, where a single individual comprises the corporation. The modern law of corporations follows the fundamental principles of the Roman law of private corporations. The modern codes have merely enlarged and broadened the rules found in the Corpus Juris.

PROPERTY AND OBLIGATIONS

The law of things as classified by Gaius and the later Roman lawyers could not bear transplanting as a body into modern systems of law. Nevertheless, this branch of the law has made more contributions to modern codes than either the law of persons or the law of actions. The difficulty of discovering relationships between the rules of ancient and modern codes, as has already been observed, arises because the Romans had not yet attained the conception of a right, which is basic to modern systems of law.

The subject matter of the law of things in Roman and modern law is property. This comprises roughly ownership, rights in the property of another, for example, servitudes or easements, and obligations, such as contracts and delicts or torts. The peculiarity of the Roman law which led to the inclusion of the law of inheritance within the law of things has no counterpart in modern codes. At Rome, the heir acceded to the personality of the deceased, assuming the liabilities as well as the assets of the estate. Justinian approved some changes in the unlimited liability of the heir for the debts of the deceased but did not approximate the situation of the modern executor or administrator.

The law of obligations formed the most important part of the law of things, because the praetor gave the greatest attention to it. The careful consideration of bona fides, or good faith, which marks the Roman law, has provided modern law with completed tasks which do not have to be done again. The classifications of obligations differ in modern and Roman systems of law, and the methods of forming and extinguishing obligations vary in modern codes. They are not always the same as in the Roman law. But the fundamental principles of the law as laboriously worked out in the court of the praetor have formed a pattern from which the makers of modern codes have not departed.

The detailed and precise contributions of the Roman law of things to the different codes of modern law cannot be set forth here. The student who wishes to make this detailed comparison must utilize the special aids which legal scholars have prepared.[4] The outcome of any such study will be a clear recognition of the debt of modern law to that of Rome.

THE LAW OF PROCEDURE

The law of actions, as defined by Gaius, took into account the legis actio procedure which had been superseded about 130 B.C. by the formulary procedure. Although the ancient legis actiones were not abolished until the time of Augustus, they were on the wane after the passage of the lex Aebutia. It is superfluous to remark that the legis actio system did not influence the development of civil procedure in modern times.

In any period the definition of an action is that given by the jurist Celsus, "nothing else than the right of an individual to sue in a trial for what is due him." In the formal sense an action embraces the right of a plaintiff by which he initiates a suit as well as the whole proceedings whereby justice is achieved.

The formulary procedure was first introduced at Rome for the benefit of foreigners and was later extended to Roman citizens. Under this procedure a litigant could be represented in court by an attorney, which had been impossible under the older system. A highly developed system of pleading was created which was accepted by Justinian and transmitted to all modern civil procedure.

The final stage in the development of the law of procedure came in the reign of Diocletian, who in 294 B.C. abolished the formula and established the extraordinary procedure. Diocletian disliked

---

[4] Students are referred especially to Vol. III of the work of Sherman and to J. Williams, *The Institutes of Justinian Illustrated by English Law* (London, 1883).

the practice of dividing the task of adjudication between the magistrate and *judex* (juror) and insisted that ordinarily the magistrate should try and decide all cases. Instead of the formula, there was substituted a written complaint and summons which informed the defendant of the nature of the lawsuit brought against him.

Diocletian was the last emperor to issue his decisions in the form of rescripts directed to all Romans and therefore possessing the form of law. The number of rescripts grew rapidly, and there exist today at least a thousand of Diocletian's rescripts. The successors of Diocletian communicated their decisions only to the parties immediately concerned. These had binding force only in a single case. When a matter had been weighed and found to have bearing upon the national interests as a whole, it was embodied in the form of a statute and promulgated by the emperor. A clear distinction was drawn between the legislative and judicial functions of the emperor. His power to create law was distinguished from his power to interpret or declare the law. Thereafter the course of legislation was to be determined, not by the accidental requirements of single cases, but by the general needs of the empire. This system of Roman procedure is that which was current in Justinian's time and underlies all modern code procedure.

Substantive law is everywhere largely the creature of procedure. When the state began to substitute for the blood feud and other forms of self-help some form of judicial procedure, it paved the way for the growth of substantive law. If the state was to decide who was to be protected it must also decide what matters were to be the subjects of protection. The foundations were thus laid for substantive law. It is not always easy to distinguish between substantive and procedural law. Where codification exists, it is the tendency for procedure to dominate the law. Indeed, the early codes from the XII Tables through the codes of barbarian law were almost entirely concerned with the forms of procedure. But the view that substantive law depends completely or even largely upon the development of procedure is today somewhat primitive and old-fashioned. Modern legislatures enact measures which can only be defined as substantive law without paying any attention to the modes of their enforcement.

The Roman element in English law is much more difficult to discover than is the case with modern continental codifications. Whereas there is at the heart of each civil law system a large body of received Roman law, this is not true of the English common law. The obvious contributions of Roman law are through the ecclesiastical, chancery, and admiralty courts. But the rules of law formulated in these courts touch only tangentially the rule of common law developed in the courts of the king. Moreover, most of the borrowings by the ecclesiastical and admiralty courts have been embodied in statute, and the chancery rules have become precedents. When reference is made to a rule of the chancery it is to the decision and not to the basis of the decision. It is therefore difficult to ascertain the original foundation of any particular doctrine in the English courts.

THE ROMAN ELEMENT IN ENGLISH LAW

Roman law has not been disdained by English judges when they were unable to find guiding principles nearer at hand. In the absence of statutory authority or applicable precedents a judge must decide a case on principle. No body of law affords a more fruitful field to the judge in search of general principles than the law of Rome. The doctrine has been stated by Tindal, C. J., in a passage which has become a classic:

The Roman law forms no rule, binding in itself, upon the subject of these realms; but, in deciding a case upon principle, where no direct authority can be cited from our books, it affords no small evidence of the soundness of the conclusion at which we have arrived, if it proves to be supported by that law, the fruits of the researches of the most learned men, the collective wisdom of the ages, and the groundwork of the municipal law of most of the countries in Europe.[5]

Since a judge always seeks the most authoritative pronouncements to support his decisions, he will not turn to a foreign system of

[5] *Acton v. Blundell*, 2 M. and W. 324 (1843).

law unless the common law and the statutes of the realm are unavailing. Modern judges may quote Roman law as dicta but they will in general endeavor, wherever possible, to keep within the range of reported decisions.

English judges are sometimes called upon to decide cases in which the rules of some other legal system are called into question. Such cases fall within the category of conflict of laws or private international law. Where such cases involve the law of some country in which there has been a more or less extensive reception of the Roman law, the judges will necessarily have recourse to the principles laid down in the Corpus Juris.

Finally, appeals to the House of Lords from Scotland and to the Judicial Committee of the Privy Council from South Africa, and other jurisdictions where the local law contains a large element of Roman origin, will compel the matter to be considered on a larger canvas than can be provided by the common law. Many of these cases have resulted in decisions in which the rules laid down were greatly at variance with those of the English common law.[6]

In the past there were two widely separated schools of writers upon the sources of English law. One regarded the common law as wholly indigenous, or at least chiefly of Teutonic origin, while the other school acknowledged the large debt which it owes to Roman law. The first came down from Coke and Hale and was best exemplified in the United States by Oliver Wendell Holmes. The second school comprised Savigny and the English students of Bracton, especially Sir Travers Twiss, the editor of the Rolls Series on Bracton.

Neither of these schools of jurists can maintain its position if carried to a logical conclusion. The debt of the common law to Roman models cannot be denied. The Romans contributed many of the terms and maxims in use by common law jurists and writers on the law. There is little doubt that Roman law had no influence

[6] These examples are taken from an excellent essay by D. T. Oliver, "Roman Law in Modern Cases in English Courts," *Cambridge Legal Essays* (Cambridge, 1926), pp. 243–257.

on English law until Vacarius came to teach in England. Bracton, who wrote almost a century later, modelled his work on the Roman law as glossed by Azo, although he insisted that he was dealing with English law as an independent system. At the same time, it is clear that Bracton was obliged to depart from his Roman patterns as his work progressed. Bracton, the judge, probably dealt with the law quite differently from Bracton, the writer. The most that can be said for dependence of English upon Roman law, apart from ecclesiastical, chancery, and admiralty jurisdictions, will give support to the claims of neither school of juristic writers. Truth in this instance will be found in some middle ground.

But the student who seeks to identify rules of Roman law with those of the common law will find guides to his research. The coincidences between Roman and English law show how numerous are the principles and distinctions which all systems of law have in common. The differences in the two systems can be ascribed in the main to the different origins of Roman and English law and to their historical development. "The theoretical descent of Roman jurisprudence from a code (the XII Tables)," Sir Henry Maine has said, "the theoretical ascription of English law to immemorial unwritten tradition, were the chief reasons why the development of their system differed from the development of ours."[7]

Furthermore, the development of the two systems has proceeded in opposite directions. The Roman law moved steadily in the direction of strengthening the power of the emperor. In the republican period, the Roman praetor had free discretion within his own court to grant or refuse an action. When he was deprived of this power through the codification of the praetorian edict by Salvius Julianus, the first step had been taken towards vesting judicial power in the emperor. The path thus marked out, emperors from the time of Hadrian did not hesitate to tread. Long before the time of Justinian, the Roman emperors had brought the interpretation as well as the making of law within their own control.

[7] H. S. Maine, *Ancient Law* (Everyman's Library ed.), Ch. I.

English law has moved in the opposite direction. The judges have been freed from the mandates of the king and are bound only by the precedents and the acts of Parliament. The proclamations of the king have not had the force of law since the sixteenth century. Indeed, since the reign of Edward I there has been a steady limitation upon the prerogatives of the Crown, although revolution has been necessary at times to accomplish the desired end.

There is much in Roman law that can find no counterpart in English law. The law of persons as outlined by Gaius cannot be discovered in English law, or in modern civil codes. Land law in England is derived from feudal institutions or from Anglo-Saxon rules prior to the teaching of Roman law at Oxford. The judicial procedure in English courts is very different from the law of actions at Rome. But the law of things, and especially the law of obligations, has helped many English judges to find principles upon the basis of which to decide cases where the statutes and prior decisions were silent. Finally, there is no part of the Roman law which has not been ransacked to find apt terms and pithy maxims with which to embellish juristic writings.

The writings of jurists have been much more important in the countries which have "received" the Roman law than in England and the United States. From the close of the Roman republic, when the Sabinians contested with the Proculians, to our own day juristic writing has sought to transform a mere knowledge of the law into legal science. English writers have attempted to do the same thing for the common law. Fortesque, Coke, Hale, and Blackstone, to mention only a few Englishmen, wrote commentaries which sought to bring philosophy and history to the interpretation of the law. But these men were judges who drew their inspiration from the cases which came before them or from the decisions of other judges who had preceded them. They were dealing with a narrow national law rather than a universal system which crossed many frontiers in Europe until it became a common law for most continental countries. The jurists on the continent have always had before them the model of the Roman law which, in the form left by Justinian, attempted to reach every phase of life to which the law could apply.

In other words, the jurist has always aimed at completeness for his system.[8] This is quite impossible for the English and American writers on the common law. They can only deal with those matters which have already come before the courts, leaving great gaps in the law as to those issues not yet brought into litigation. The continental jurist, on the other hand, is able to keep the law ahead of the facts. The glossators and their successors, working out the implications of the law contained in the Corpus Juris, frequently discussed the solutions to problems which had not yet arisen.

It is perhaps worth while to observe that in civil law jurisdictions the judge tends more and more to depart from the strict letter of the code and to make law in a way no English or American judge would do at the present time. On the other hand, common law judges in England and the United States have been departing from precedents. The doctrine of *stare decisis* is wearing thin. Judges do not follow precedents which time has shown to be lacking in logic and common sense. Common law judges will follow the sound precedents wherever possible, but no judge will court a reversal on appeal by adopting a rule which is obviously inadequate to meet a situation which confronts him.

In conclusion, it may be stated that there has never been a time since the Middle Ages when Roman law has failed to influence the development of law in England as well as on the continent. Continental systems, as has been observed, contain large bodies of received Roman law. Much of this is in Bartolist form. That is to say, it is Roman law as adapted by the commentators to the requirements of the courts. But, as John Austin has pointed out, there are coincidences as well as differences among all systems of law. The English common law is no exception.[9]

[8] See on this general topic F. H. Lawson, *A Common Lawyer Looks at the Civil Law* (Ann Arbor, 1955).

[9] T. F. T. Plucknett, *Concise History of the Common Law,* 4th ed. (London, 1948), pp. 282–284.

The influence of Roman law upon Bracton was greater than its influence upon the common law of his time. But when Bracton's book was first printed in the sixteenth century, judges turned to his pages to help them in expanding the common law. There was no danger that the Roman law would supplant the common law either in the time of Bracton or in a later day. Because the common law was so firmly established in judicial precedents, the English judges may well have read Bracton in order to aid them in understanding their own law and to bring solutions to unsettled questions. Roman law in the terms used by Bracton may today influence judges who cannot elsewhere find adequate guidance.

XI

The Growth of English Law

THE GROWTH OF ENGLISH LAW in modern times must be studied in the field of legislation. Statute law on both sides of the Atlantic contains the key to legal development since the eighteenth century. The tremendous output of statutory enactments in the reign of Edward I was unmatched until the nineteenth century. In the meantime the system of government in England was to undergo almost complete transformation.

Edward I was still within the Middle Ages; legislative acts ran in the name of the king and were probably initiated by him or one of his councillors. Some of the most important legislation was enacted without reference to the House of Commons. There is, however, no legal difference in effect or authority of statutes produced in different ways. The Statute of Westminster II appears to have proceeded from the king in council, whereas other legislative enactments involved consultation of the king with the nobles and commons of the realm in Parliament.[1] A statute in the reign of

[1] T. F. T. Plucknett, *Concise History of the Common Law*, 4th ed. (London, 1948), p. 304.

Edward I means merely something established by royal authority.

Parliament did not for several centuries after Edward I become the omnipotent and omnicompetent authority lauded by Blackstone.[1a] It did not attempt to control the common law, but left this to the judges and the lawyers. Indeed, there was little legislation of great significance, the Statute of Uses excepted, to which Parliament could lay claim until after 1660. There was an abundance of statutory law enacted with reference to matters of small and transient importance. While all acts, great and small, were done by the authority of Parliament, the legislation of importance was passed in subservience to the Crown.

Nevertheless, the amount of statute law became so great that revision engaged the attention of the Crown at an early date. In 1551 the young King Edward VI wrote a *Discourse on the Reformation of Abuses* in which he said: "I have shewed my opinion heretofore what statutes I think most necessary to be enacted this session. Nevertheless, I would wish that beside them hereafter, when time shall serve, the superfluous and tedious statutes were brought into one sum together, and made more plain and short, to the intent that men might better understand them; which thing shall much help to advance the profit of the Commonwealth." Nothing came of this suggestion, nor did a more elaborate proposal in the reign of Elizabeth by Sir Nicholas Bacon for the "reducing, ordering, and printing the statutes of the realm" meet with success.[2]

[1a] There are several good histories of English law, the most extensive being that of William S. Holdsworth, *History of English Law*, 13 vol. (London, 1922–1952).

The *Short History of English Law* by Edward Jenks, 2nd ed. (Boston, 1922) is excellent but too technical for most college students. Oliver Wendell Holmes, *The Common Law* (Boston, 1881), while not a history and written many years ago, is helpful to students seeking an analysis of the English law. A more recent book by John Chipman Gray, *Nature and Sources of the Law* (New York, 1909) is first-rate for beginning students, although again it is not a historical study. It may be, as Maitland once said, that a history of English law will never be written.

[2] C. Ilbert, *The Mechanics of Law Making* (New York, 1914). p. 25.

In the reign of James I, efforts were made by the Crown to secure substantial revision of the statutes. Sir Francis Bacon, the Attorney-General, made the following proposals to the king, "touching the compiling and amendment of the laws of England:"

For the reforming and recompiling of the statute law, it consisteth of four parts.

1. The Government to discharge the books of those statutes wherein the case by alteration of time is vanished, as Lombards, Jews, Gauls, halfpence, etc. Those may, nevertheless, remain in the libraries for antiquities, but no reprinting of them. The like of statutes long since expired and clearly repealed; for if the repeal be doubtful, it must so be propounded by Parliament.

2. The next is to repeal all statutes which are sleeping and not of use, but yet snaring and in force. In some of those it will perhaps be requisite to substitute some more reasonable law instead of them, agreeable to the time; in others a simple repeal may suffice.

3. The third, that the grievousness of the penalty in many statutes may be mitigated, though the ordinance stand.

4. The last is the reducing of convenient statutes heaped one upon another to one clear and uniform law.[3]

These praiseworthy objectives were not attained until after the eighteenth century, although several committees appear to have been set up from time to time to deal with the matter. The reason for this lag in statute law must be sought in the constitutional crises which arose in England in the seventeenth century.

INFLUENCE OF CONSTITUTIONAL CHANGES IN ENGLAND

The seventeenth century in England was a period of revolution in which two conceptions of the constitution struggled for supremacy. It has been described as a contest between the personal monarchy of the Stuart kings and the representatives of the people in the House of Commons. The contest had its religious as well

[3] *Ibid.*, pp. 26–27.

as political aspects, but at the bottom it was a difference of opinion as to the location of sovereign power.

At the height of the struggle, Thomas Hobbes defined law as the command of the sovereign. This definition swept away the cobwebs which had surrounded the definition of law in earlier generations. Divine law and natural law were absorbed in the rules which the sovereign might lay down as civil law. It was one thing to say that law is what the sovereign commands and another to say who was the sovereign. The latter task could not be accomplished by a paper shot from the ivory tower of a political philosopher. The precise location of sovereign power remained for the clash of arms to settle.

The personal rule of the Stuart kings ended when Charles I ascended the scaffold. In other words, no king could thereafter govern England without the consent and cooperation of Parliament. Whether Parliament could rule without a king was another matter. From the execution of Charles I to the restoration of Charles II was a period in which England came perilously close to anarchy. Parliament controlled the course of English affairs for twenty years, from 1640 to 1660, with some interruptions, just as Charles I had been in control of them for the preceding fifteen years. The military dictatorship which Oliver Cromwell and the army set up could not survive its leader. When the Protectorate fell within a year after the death of Cromwell, the monarchy was restored under Charles II.

The restoration of the monarchy in 1660 established Charles II in a different form of kingship than his father had inherited from James I and which he had vainly striven to uphold. Although the dogma of divine right of kings was preached from pulpits and taught through pamphlets in every part of England, the king could not have acted upon the principles outlined by James I in his *True Law of Free Monarchies*. Charles II was a constitutional monarch in the sense that he was obliged to observe constitutional forms from which he could not depart. Except for his insistence that his brother inherit the throne as James II, the king yielded to the wishes of Parliament or took refuge in secret or underhand attempts to oppose it. In other words, the supremacy of Parliament was acknowledged and has existed to the present time.

The restoration of Charles II was not only a restoration of the hereditary heir to the throne but also a restoration of Parliament, of the established church, and of old customs. At the outset the religious aspect of the restoration did not attract attention, because the king was genuinely in favor of toleration. But Parliament in 1673 forced the issue by requiring that nobody should hold office under the government who would not first declare his disbelief in the doctrine of transubstantiation and receive the sacrament of communion according to the rites of the church of England. The supremacy of the established church was not complete.

James II became king, in spite of efforts in Parliament to exclude him. The objections to James sprang from the fact that he had become a communicant in the Catholic church. This was hateful not only to Parliament but also to a majority of the people of England. It is probable that James could have maintained himself on the throne for a reign which, because of his age, would necessarily be short, if he had proceeded with wisdom and tact. Unfortunately, he chose to reassert many of the principles which had been negated in the reign of Charles I. The unpopularity of James was widespread, but direct action against him was not undertaken because his eldest daughter Mary, the wife of William of Orange, was expected to succeed him. England would then have a Protestant ruler whose husband was a distinguished general and an able administrator who could be expected to give sound guidance to the Crown. These rosy expectations were dispelled by the birth of a male heir to James and his wife. Since the heir would undoubtedly be brought up in the Catholic faith, the people of England saw no advantage in waiting for better times. They could not endure the prospect of a line of Catholic rulers.

Informal negotiations were opened with William of Orange to come to England and preserve its liberties against the attacks of the king. In pursuance of these requests, William landed in England on November 5, 1688, with an army of fourteen thousand men and marched toward London. James marched with an army to meet him but soon found that he had been deserted by nearly all his previous supporters. The king attempted no further resistance but arranged to flee to France on the same day that William took up his dwelling at Whitehall.

For the moment there was no government; England was subject to an armed invader. But the constitutional issue was settled by summoning a convention similar to that which had invited Charles II to the throne. When this convention had assembled, it passed a bill offering the crown to William and Mary as joint sovereigns, the administration of the government to be in the hands of William. At the same time, the convention enumerated the grievances against the former king and stated that they expected the new king and queen to agree to the parliamentary view of them. William and Mary accepted the crown on these terms and were proclaimed king and queen of England on February 13, 1689.

When the new king and queen had been crowned, they transformed the convention into a regular Parliament, and it proceeded to pass various bills. The most important of these was the Bill of Rights, which was a re-enactment in statutory form of the declaration of rights accepted the year before by William and Mary as conditions attached to their occupying the throne. The Bill of Rights of 1689 should be classed with the Great Charter of 1215 and the Petition of Right of 1629 as the three most important and fundamental documents which define the English constitution.

The supremacy of Parliament was complete. As a result of the revolutions of the seventeenth century it was made apparent that the English people had in their hands the power and the right to set up forms of government to their fancy. Parliament with popular approval had brought back one king and then obliged his successor to abdicate. It had set up William and Mary and declared the legitimacy of their rule. Finally, in 1701 it had by the Act of Settlement not only limited the descent of the Crown but also added a few constitutional provisions supplementary to those of the Bill of Rights. At the same time that the Crown was subordinated to Parliament, the constitution began to be overlaid by political practices that created working relationships among the different branches of the government. Although the veto ceased to be used in the reign of Anne, a nice poise and balance was established between the Crown, the House of Lords, and House of Commons through customary procedures and statutory enactments.

The resurgence of Parliament led to the rapid growth of statute law. By the time of Charles II the common law had taken its permanent shape and its principles were made available in printed reports. Whereas before 1648 there were only the Year Books and some commentaries and abridgments, the next century saw a large number of reports of cases, both at law and equity. The courts of equity, having been freed from subservience to the king, could join with the legislature in the task of improving and supplementing the common law.

The legal reforms of the reign of Charles II were highlighted by the Statute of Frauds (1677) and the Habeas Corpus Act (1679). The first of these acts was designed to avoid perjury and subornation of perjury by requiring a written form for certain contracts, leases, and wills. The Habeas Corpus Act stems from the thirty-ninth clause of Magna Carta, by which the king undertook that no free man should be imprisoned otherwise than by the judgment of his peers, or by the law of the land. The provisions of the act passed in the reign of Charles II enabled a person held in custody to have himself brought promptly before a court to determine the reason for his detention.

Less spectacular than these statutes were acts abolishing medieval land tenures. Many features of feudal landholding had long ceased to be observed, but the laws governing them continued in force. By the legislation signed by Charles II the feudal land law was swept away. Thus, at the moment when Parliament was acting to guarantee greater freedom to Englishmen under the common law it was also removing from the common law many rules which, had they been enforced, would have restricted the personal freedom of the subject.

The history of English legislation during the eighteenth century is almost a blank. Few laws of any significance were placed upon the statute book. But that is not to say there was no legal reform. The equity courts took up the task of improving and supplementing the law during the period following the revolution of 1688. Whether this was because the people of England distrusted the rough and clumsy methods of legislation, or whether they were bewildered by the changes in agriculture and industry and uncertain what action to take, cannot be said. Certainly the industrial revolution created problems which makers of statutes could not foresee. The enactment of a sound statute requires that there shall be some permanence and stability in the subject matter to which it applies. In the parliamentary environment of the eighteenth century, no analysis of economic or political trends in the country was possible.

Parliament was comprised largely of country gentlemen. Legislation was the work of amateurs, not of specialists. The lawyers who might be expected to give leadership in any movement of legal reform were so closely identified by ties of blood or marraige with the gentry that they were unable to look beyond tradition and were content with things as they found them. The country squire had strong prejudices, but he also had sense enough to recognize his own ignorance. For the law itself he had the profound veneration, which is expressed by Blackstone. The common law was a tradition, not made by express legislation. Any gaps could best be filled up by judicial interpretation. Had not Lord Mansfield and his colleagues on the court of king's bench developed the commercial law to meet all requirements? Parliament was content not to act while, as they thought, the judges with popular approval were moving so successfully to keep the law abreast of changing social and economic conditions.

Thus matters stood in 1776, the *annus mirabilis*, when the American Declaration of Independence was hurled at George III, and the *Wealth of Nations* of Adam Smith and the *Fragment on Government* of Jeremy Bentham first appeared. The last of these publications proved in some respects to be as revolutionary as the first. Although it did not lose for England a great colonial empire, it did herald the advent of scientific methods which were to change radically the field of legislation. The *Fragment on Government* was a powerful attack upon Blackstone. Its biting criticism of the glorification of the common law as set forth in the *Commentaries* would alone have compelled a further examination of judge-made law. But Bentham was not satisfied with destructive criticism; he never attacked an abuse without also outlining the remedy. Precedent was not the Benthamite form of law. The only proper source of law to Bentham was legislation.[4]

BENTHAMITE REFORMS

Benthamism was made to rest upon a fundamental principle which its founder believed to be unassailable. "It is the greatest happiness of the greatest number that is the measure of right and wrong," declared Bentham. When his attention was called to the writers of the *Federalist*, who saw justice as the end of government, Bentham replied: "Why not happiness? What happiness is every man knows, because what pleasure is, every man knows, and what pain is, every man knows. But what justice is—this is what on every occasion is the subject-matter of dispute."[5] There could be no clearer or more concise statement of the foundations of Benthamism. All the reasoning of Bentham and all of his devices for the reform of law and politics were designed to achieve the greatest happiness for the greatest number.

Through a kind of felicific calculus, Bentham believed the legislator could arrive at conclusions upon the basis of which to frame and pass a bill. By calculating in terms of pains and pleasures the

---

[4] For a study of Bentham and his school, see Leslie Stephen, *The English Utilitarians*, 3 vol. (New York, 1900).

[5] *Ibid.*, I, p. 238.

effect of a proposed measure, the legislator can determine to pass the bill when the pleasures to be derived outweigh the pains caused. The method was useful in the civil as well as the criminal law. The classifications essential to the method were published in 1817 by James Mill as the *Table of the Springs of Action*. While this curious publication was soon forgotten, the type of reasoning it exemplifies was to color legal thought throughout the greater part of the nineteenth century.

The practical applications of Benthamism were made by the disciples of Bentham. John Austin laid the foundations of the analytical school of jurisprudence which has held a commanding position to our own day. Romilly and Brougham took into the House of Commons the principles laid down by the master to reform the government and to improve legislation. Codification, Bentham reserved to himself. To the end of his life Bentham sat in his study writing codes in which he sought to prescribe for all the evils of the time. This phase of Benthamism attracted much greater attention on the European continent than in England.

The adoption of the Reform Bill of 1832 was a triumph for the Benthamites. The bill broadened the franchise and destroyed the representation of many special interests. The reform of Parliament was followed by a wave of reform legislation. The leaders in the House of Commons had in the felicific calculus a method of political reasoning which enabled them to deal with many social problems which had long awaited solution. The Municipal Corporations Act of 1835 introduced into the government of towns and cities changes which placed the control of affairs in the hands of all property owners. The Factory Act of 1833 restricted the employment of children in factories and provided that factory inspectors be appointed to enforce the law. Although factory laws had been in existence for some years, the act of 1833 proved to be the forerunner of much legislation which not only extended the protection of the state to women and children in industry but also provided for its enforcement. The Poor Law Act of 1834 repealed the poor law which had existed since the reign of Elizabeth and substituted a number of provisions designed to care for paupers at the same time that they put to work the able-bodied recipients of poor relief. These were some of the outstanding legislative enactments ment to insure the greatest happiness for the greatest number. Recourse to legislation having again been undertaken, the statute book was soon beginning to fill up with enactments, until the number in a single year exceeded the whole of a medieval reign.

The argument from a priori conceptions of human nature, which characterized all the followers of Bentham, has been vigorously criticized. Since Jevons showed the way to the compilation of statistical data as the basis for legislation, statesmen have more and more tended to disdain the older method of political reasoning. Nevertheless, a mere statistical datum remains a dumb thing until the human mind brings it to life in an important way. Statistics are undoubtedly more valuable than the *Table of the Springs of Action*, but they must be interpreted in the light of human needs and human nature before they can be helpful in drafting a statute. There is no evidence that modern legislators are more skillful in adapting the materials of their political reasoning to the solution of current problems than were the Benthamites in the 1830's. The data with which the modern legislator works are more precise and more abundant, but the conclusions which he reaches are not always more successful. Much depends upon the intelligence of the legislators and the quality of their leadership. One cannot expect good legislation without good legislators.

REVIVAL OF LEGISLATION

But it cannot be denied that in modern times the growth of the law depends upon legislation. Oliver Wendell Holmes said:

In substance the growth of the law is legislative. The very considerations which judges most rarely mention, and always with an apology, are the secret root from which the law draws all the juices of life. I mean, of course, considerations of what is expedient for the community concerned. Every important principle which is developed by litigation is in fact and at bottom the result of more or less definitely understood views of public policy; most generally, to be sure, under our practice and traditions, the unconscious result of instinctive preferences and inarticulate convictions, but none the less traceable to views of public policy in the last analysis.[6]

In other words, it is the legislator who must formulate public policy and give it practical form in a statute. In so doing, he finds it necessary to take into account conflicting opinions in the community of what the law should embrace.

Finally, the judge must interpret the statute when it is brought before him in the course of litigation. He must not only decide what the statute means but must also fill in the cracks and crannies which appear in much statute law. Sometimes the judge is required to find meaning in a statute when none was intended by the legislature. It has not been unknown for a legislature to pass bills hastily with insufficient consideration and leave to the courts the refinement of its product. Fortunately, with modern improvements in legislative techniques, the occasions when this is done have become less frequent. But whether it is admitted or not, judges engage in legislation. It is, perhaps, superfluous to remark that what judges say in their opinions influences profoundly the course of subsequent legislation.

The trend in legislation, as Dicey has pointed out, has been toward collectivism.[7] In other words, the individualism of the Benthamite era has given place to a socialism which regards the state as the protector and guardian of all its citizens. It is not enough for the state to insure each individual the opportunity to determine his own social and economic destiny, it must assume the direct responsibility for the welfare or happiness of every citizen.

The new climate of opinion was first clearly shown in Mr. Forster's Elementary Education Act of 1870. For the first time, the state assumed a definite responsibility for the education of children

[6] *The Common Law,* pp. 35–36.
[7] A. V. Dicey, *Law and Public Opinion in England,* 2nd ed. (London, 1926).

whose parents were unable to pay school fees. By 1891, elementary education had become free. From education, Parliament passed on to labor. Earlier labor legislation was designed to prevent exploitation of children in large factories. But the acts which began in 1878 and culminated in the Factory and Workshop Act of 1906 intervened to procure the proper management of shops. Meanwhile, state regulation of trade unions was by statute brought from the strict prohibitions of the combination law of 1800 to the favorable legislation of the last half century whereby, in the opinion of many persons, workingmen have been placed not merely on a basis of equality but even of privilege with employers. Perhaps there are no better examples than the labor laws to show the reflection of public opinion in the law.

Any catalogue of bills introduced in parliament during the last eighty years will show the growth of socialistic sentiments. That is to say, social interests rather than individual rights condition the legislation of the present. Said Dean Pound:

In the last century, legal history was written as a record of the unfolding of individual freedom, as a record of continually increasing recognition and securing of individual interests, through the pressure, as it were, of the individual will. But it would be quite as easy to write it in terms of a continually wider and broader recognition and securing of social interests, that is, of the claims and demands involved in the existence of civilized society, not the least of which is the social interest in the individual human life.[8]

Whether the growth of English law in recent times be studied as the unfolding of the freedom of the human will or the greater recognition of social interests, the form it takes is statute law. This is a development of modern times. The Romans resorted seldom to the legislature, regarding statute law (*lex*) as essential only when emergencies arose which could not otherwise be met. Earlier generations of Englishmen distrusted legislation and depended upon the lawyers and judges to shape the law. Benthamism changed this

[8] R. Pound, *Interpretations of Legal History* (New York, 1923), p. 163.

210

and centered attention upon legislation as a source of law and a remedy for evils.

Revolutionary changes have not followed recourse to legislation in England or the United States. This has not always been true in countries on the continent of Europe, where statutory enactments have sometimes led to sanguinary uprisings. The reason for the ready acceptance of most legislative acts in England and America is not hard to find. There is nothing spasmodic or reckless about Anglo-American legislation. There is ordinarily a fully matured legislative policy from which statutes are the logical outcome. The enactment of a statute in England and the United States is the final step in a process which began when public opinion on the subject was first crystallized. This process is sometimes called one of education. Legislation which proves defective or unworkable is usually the result of inadequate attention to the path men have trod to bring others to realize the need for action.

XII

Some Recent Trends
in Jurisprudence

THE PAST HALF CENTURY has been a period of turmoil in world
affairs. Two world wars and a world-wide economic depression
have followed the quiet times of the nineteenth century. This un-
rest has penetrated the field of jurisprudence, where leading jurists
have been querying and contesting the most fundamental doctrines
of the theory of law. While re-examination of established notions
is from time to time highly desirable, this should lead to systematic improvements of the law. Much good work is being done,
but contemporary jurists would hardly agree that great progress
has been made.[1]

Progress depends upon fundamental agreement not only as to
objectives to be attained but also as to methods to be pursued.
There has been no controversy over the aims and purposes of juris-

[1] Periodical literature must necessarily supply most of the materials for any
study of contemporary activities in the field of jurisprudence. Articles in
legal periodicals will be found through the use of the *Index to Legal Periodicals.*

prudence, these are primarily an attempt to formulate in general terms the ideals and purposes of the law at a particular period. Differences among students of the subject turn upon the methods most appropriate to achieve the objectives. In the social sciences it is not enough for people to know what they want; they must also know how to get it.

CONTRIBUTIONS OF THE SCHOOLS OF JURISPRUDENCE

The great contribution of John Austin and the analytical school of jurisprudence was the application of logic to the problems of the law. This led to the development of a rigid system in which sole reliance was placed upon deductive reasoning. Experience was discarded, with the result that jurisprudence became almost as sterile as the scholastic philosophy of the Middle Ages. But, like the scholastic philosophy, the analytical school of jurisprudence had its uses. English jurists have continued to believe that problems of analysis, clarification, and definition remain the hard core of jurisprudence.[2] They have abandoned the rigid system of Austin but have held fast to the fundamental requirements of his method.

The fundamental mistake made by Austin was that he regarded law as a mere aggregation of rules. This is a mistake common to jurists who are content to follow the Hobbesian definition of law as the command of the sovereign. It is a theory of law which holds good only for the legal system of a country where the sovereign is plainly discoverable. When Austin found himself unable to discover the location of sovereignty in the United States, he apparently decided not to publish during his lifetime a second edition of his *Lectures on Jurisprudence*.[3] His followers have not been more successful than the master in fashioning some important instruments of research into a system of jurisprudence capable of

[2] H. L. A. Hart, "Philosophy of Law and Jurisprudence in Britain, 1945–1952," *American Journal of Comparative Law*, II, pp. 355–364.
[3] F. S. C. Northrop, "Contemporary Jurisprudence and International Law," *Yale Law Journal*, 61, p. 625.

universal application. The techniques of the analytical school are available to jurists for whatever use they may wish to make of them, but they cannot of themselves tell the story of the origin and growth of the law. As Dean Pound has said, "the textbook of analytical jurisprudence is a legal herbarium."[4]

The Austinian school of jurisprudence has suffered from the decline of the concept of sovereignty in modern political theory. The concept has not only been challenged as lacking validity in the modern world but has also been impugned as an attempt to generalize from a single particular. Sovereignty, said Sir Frederick Pollock, is "a generalization from the 'omnipotence' of the British Parliament, an attribute which has been the offspring of our particular history, and may quite possibly suffer some considerable change in times not far distant."[5] It should be observed that sovereignty has declined in importance but has not disappeared from political theory. Much remains which cannot be explained without recourse to the concept of sovereignty. Legal writers have vainly sought to pass from the state to its institutions without the intermediary step of locating sovereignty in the state. Definition is not all that is required to establish a system of jurisprudence but one can hardly be created without the precision of exact terms.

Recognition that definition is not enough to establish a system of jurisprudence of universal application has accompanied the work of the comparative jurists. These men have broadened the scope of their activities to embrace the civilians as well as the common lawyers. But the results have thus far been disappointing. Instead of making systematic comparative studies of Roman and English law, many of these jurists have spent their time seeking contrasts between rules in the two systems.

The danger to be averted has been correctly apprehended by the comparative jurists themselves. Upon the inauguration of the

[4] R. Pound, *Interpretations of Legal History* (New York, 1923), p. 130.
[5] E. Jenks, *The New Jurisprudence* (London, 1933), p. 84.

American Journal of Comparative Law its sponsors remarked:

> It is fortunately becoming increasingly recognized that what must be compared, if comparisons are to be relevant and useful, is not doctrine merely but doctrine and practice, not a flow of rules merely, but a flow of *decisions*. Comparison cannot relevantly and usefully be confined to rules alone both because rules are not the only variables that affect decisions and because, as embodiments of policy crystallizations of the past, they may not offer adequate description of the effects of new decisions.

In other words, the purposes of comparative jurisprudence cannot be achieved without the study of the experience at Rome and in England which brought about the rules under contemplation.

Unfortunately the study of Roman law has declined in England, and in the United States has disappeared almost entirely. Few graduates of American law schools are aware of the Roman system beyond a slight acquaintance with the Institutes. On the European continent the civilians busy themselves with their codes, ignoring the rich heritage which lies behind the principles with which they deal. Modern jurists often forget that a knowledge of the classical Roman law is as important to an understanding of present day legal systems as a knowledge of Latin is to the understanding of Romance languages. The revival of the classical Roman law is a necessary prelude to the development of comparative jurisprudence.

But this may not be enough. Comparative jurisprudence has been content heretofore to confine its studies to Roman and English systems, because most of the world is governed by derivations from the law of Rome or of England. There are, however, about sixteen different legal systems throughout the civilized world which were derived neither from Roman or English law. The time is probably not far distant when the comparative jurist must raise his sights to include other systems of law previously neglected.

Comparative jurisprudence proposes to make use of the methods and contributions of all the social sciences. In other words, it seeks

FOUNDATIONS OF MODERN JURISPRUDENCE

to comprehend the human experience from which the rules of law under contemplation arise. Unlike the Bartolists, who assumed that all social science was comprised within the law, jurists of the comparative school turn to political science, economics, sociology, and anthropology to obtain guidance in the improvement of the law. Throughout their work the history of institutions plays an important part, and in recent years comparative jurists have drawn heavily upon sociology to perfect their techniques.

It may be said that comparative jurisprudence is as old as Aristotle and can claim Machiavelli and Montesquieu as exponents,[6] but the modern adherents of the school will be found subsequent to World War I. Alliances were formed during the great struggle of 1914–1918 which led to the unification of ideas across national boundaries. That is not to say, however, that a general unification of the laws of the countries of the civilized world is either possible or desirable, but steps have been taken toward bringing together for comparative study rules which have been developed in a number of legal systems.[7] This is comparative law rather than comparative jurisprudence. Nevertheless, the development of the comparative method may be expected to insure the rise of a jurisprudence in which the aims and purposes of the law will be broadly construed.

Comparative jurisprudence inevitably stimulates the critical powers of the human mind at the same time that it offers a broader scope for the accumulation of data. At no time in the history of the western world has there been a greater opportunity than at present for the development of the comparative method. Ancient and medieval societies lacked the means of rapid communication which today abound in all parts of the world. From the Peace of Westphalia in 1648 to the end of the nineteenth century the spirit of nationalism led men of each country to stand aloof from their neighbors and to disdain the help which might come to them from

[6] P. Vinogradoff, *Historical Jurisprudence* (London, 1920), I, p. 67.
[7] Jenks, *op. cit.* pp. 63–5.

abroad. But in our own day international intercourse is the normal state of affairs, which nobody can avoid. It is therefore highly desirable that the exchange of ideas among civilized peoples should lead to comparative studies of the rules of law and the experiences out of which different systems of law have arisen.

History must perform a wholly different service from that sought by the historical school of jurisprudence. Henry Sumner Maine blazed a trail which has had few followers. His pioneer work has led to legal history rather than jurisprudence. This undoubtedly was not what Maine expected. But in his history of institutions, with all its defects, Maine showed that social and political history can be of inestimable value to the students of jurisprudence. The work of the historical school of jurisprudence has not been without value because it pointed to the importance of knowledge of the life and customs of people in the distant past. Jurisprudence can never again be separated from the heritage of the past which is to be found in recorded history.

At the same time, history must be given a broad scope. Less attention to chronology is required, and more intelligent scrutiny of all the aspects of particular epochs from the time of the Greeks to the present is essential. It is idle for historians to claim that they have solved all problems with which they deal, when they have only presented accounts of the conditions under which these problems arose. Great improvements have been made in historical research during the past two centuries. The work of the historian can render powerful assistance to the jurist; it cannot give final answers to the problems of jurisprudence.

Impatience with the methods of the historian has in our own day led to the development within the social science field of behavioral studies. The scholars who are pursuing the behavioral approach have erected an elaborate cognitive behavior structure through which to reconstruct the "psychological" or "behavioral" environment within which particular decisions have been reached or specific actions taken in the past. The question has been raised "whether a formalized analytical system . . . is more effective than the unstructured, more 'intuitive' methods which historians have traditionally preferred."[8] Certainly the qualifications which the behaviorists indicate to be essential to their method of study are precisely those which a sound historian possesses. It seems doubtful whether the behaviorists can do more than provide checks upon the work of the historians.

Recourse to sociology in the study of jurisprudence has emphasized the social character of law and has given assurance that it can be improved by intelligent human effort. The sociologists, unlike the historians, have not claimed that their techniques provide final answers to the problems of human affairs. On the contrary, they have with modesty offered their aid to the other social sciences as a means of arriving at tenable conclusions. The sociologists realize that the events in human affairs do not recur in cycles but in infinite combinations. Sociology has not yet established a school of jurisprudence; it has thus far been only a method. The extreme dogmatism of the analytical school is avoided at the same time that the extravagant claims of the historians are denied.

The fundamental principles of the sociological method were derived from Montesquieu. "Laws, in their widest meaning," he wrote in *L'Esprit des Lois*, "are the necessary relations from the nature of things."[9] By this statement he meant that all laws, whether physical or positive, spring not from caprice but are the assertion of cause and effect. Positive laws are determined in large part by human reason. Nevertheless, these must be framed in relation to the characteristics of each nation.

They should be adapted in such a manner to the people for whom they are framed that it should be a great chance if those of one nation suit another. They should be in relation to the nature and principles of each government whether they form it, as may be said of politic

[8] H. and M. Sprout, *Man-Milieu Relationship Hypotheses in the Context of International Politics* (Princeton, 1956), p. 68.
[9] Book I, Ch. I.

laws; or whether they support it, as in the case of civil institutions. They should be in relation to the climate of each country, to the quality of its soil, to its situation and extent, to the principal occupation of the natives, whether husbandmen, huntsmen, or shepherds; they should have relation to the degree of liberty which the constitution will bear; to the religion of the inhabitants, to their inclinations, riches, numbers, commerce, manners, and customs.[10]

The lesson to be learned from Montesquieu is that "there is not one best form of state or constitution: no law is good or bad in the abstract. Every law, civil and political, must be considered in its relation to the environment...."[11] While Montesquieu was opposing the natural law theorists, he was at the same time laying the foundations for comparative and sociological studies in jurisprudence.

The growth of sociology was furthered tremendously in the nineteenth century by the work of Comte and Herbert Spencer, although neither man was primarily interested in law. The German jurist Jhering was the first to undertake appreciably a sociological treatment of legal facts. Lester Ward, the American sociologist, brought the ideas of Europeans, especially those of Gumplowicz, to the United States where they influenced in succeeding years the thought of many jurists.[12] But it is in the writings of Roscoe Pound that jurisprudence has profited chiefly from the sociological method.

A voluminous writer,[13] Pound never attempted to develop a neat and rigidly precise statement of the program of sociological jurisprudence.[14] That would have damaged the method he sought to establish. Just as Pound took satisfaction in the variety of methods used in teaching at the Harvard Law School, his conception of

10 *Ibid.*, Ch. III.

11 *Persian Letters* (Eng. trans.), p. 190.

12 H. Cairns, *Law and the Social Sciences* (New York, 1935), Ch. IV.

13 F. C. Setaro, *Bibliography of the Writings of Roscoe Pound* (Cambridge, Mass., 1942).

14 H. G. Reuschlein, *Jurisprudence—Its American Prophets* (Indianapolis, 1951), pp. 128 *ff.*

jurisprudence embraced all the approaches which offered something of value to the science as a whole. At the same time he denied that any one approach could be pursued to the exclusion of all others. Throughout his work Pound insists that jurisprudence shall look beyond the rules of law and the rights which they safeguard to the interests which are to be protected.

An examination of Pound's writings reveals an enormous knowledge of the heritage of the past contained in legal literature. Pound began his teaching as a young man in the University of Nebraska with a course on Roman law, a subject which continued to fascinate him throughout his later years. At various times he offered courses in the civil law, particularly as this system influenced legal development in the United States. All the while that Pound was teaching and practicing law he read the German jurists who were influencing the growth of legal thinking. But it was to Oliver Wendell Holmes, who was soon to become a leading member of the United States Supreme Court, that Pound gave credit for shaping his own approach to jurisprudence. Writing to Holmes in 1919, Pound said: "Many years ago your epoch-making address on The Path of the Law won me over to this functional conception of jurisprudence, and I am more convinced that it represents the side of legal science upon which we must chiefly insist."[15]

For Pound the functional approach to jurisprudence meant the balancing of conflicting interests and securing the satisfaction of the maximum of wants with the minimum of friction. Some critics have deplored the use of the word *sociological* to describe Pound's method of study,[16] but there is no term which states precisely the intellectual breadth of this encyclopedic teacher and writer. A somewhat narrower view of the law has been taken by the left wing of the functional school comprised of men who have been called realists. With these jurists, Pound has sometimes agreed and at other times has been in sharp disagreement.

[15] P. Sayre, *Life of Roscoe Pound* (Iowa City, 1948), p. 276.
[16] G. W. Paton, *Textbook of Jurisprudence* (Oxford, 1946), p. 18.

THE NEO-REALIST MOVEMENT

The realists do not form a school of jurisprudence; they exist only as individuals who assume a common approach to problems of law, and their method has been said to be that of realism. The realists claim Justice Holmes as their mentor. In the same address which inspired Pound to follow the functional approach, Holmes said: "The prophesies of what the courts will do in fact, and nothing more pretentious, are what I mean by the law.[17] Following this precept, the realists emphasize what the judge does rather than what he says. Impulse and instinct become more important in framing judicial opinions than principles derived from a long line of precedents.

Jerome Frank, a leader among the realists, in a brilliant book entitled *Law and the Modern Mind*[18] contrasts appearance and reality in law. Borrowing from the techniques of psychoanalysis and applying these to the law, Judge Frank seeks to banish the myth that law can be entirely predictable. The law, for Judge Frank, consists of judicial decisions in which there can be no certainty, because a judge's decisions are the outcome of his entire life history.[19] Prejudices of which the judge may likely be unaware enter into the making of every opinion. The judge is expected to dispose of litigation, not to formulate rules and principles. The law is therefore the individual decision and not a system of general rules and principles.[20] A science of jurisprudence, if it is to exist at all, must be constructed of other materials than the precedents and principles of the jurists which Judge Frank has consigned to the dustbin.

Perhaps better known among American jurists than Judge Frank is Professor Karl N. Llewellyn, whose writings over the years have

[17] O. W. Holmes, *Collected Papers* (New York, 1920), pp. 167–202.
[18] (New York, 1930).
[19] *Law and the Modern Mind*, Ch. XII.
[20] Reuschlein, pp. 183–275.

greatly strengthened the position of the realists.[21] There are peculiarities of terminology in Llewellyn's work, but he has stated the practical purpose of the law more succinctly than others in the realist movement. His most important service to jurisprudence was his vindication of Sir Henry Maine's proposition that the judge goes before the law. Llewellyn drew heavily on the Cheyenne Indians, the study of whose institutions led him to his concept of the source of law.[22] Conflicts in society, according to Llewellyn, are not resolved by words and rules but by officials. "What these officials do about disputes," he said, "is, to my mind, the law itself."[23] What the judge is going to do in deciding a case before him is much more important than any rule he may cite to sustain his action. He has a choice of precedents, sometimes a wide choice, but he can do only one thing in any individual case. It is what the judge does that becomes the law.

The realists cannot be dismissed out of hand, because they attack the principles, rules, and concepts of the law, which are the subject matter of jurisprudence. It would be unfair to charge them with seeking to substitute judgment by whimsey for the settled principles which are a part of our legal heritage. What they have done is to emphasize the part played by the judge in lawmaking. Indeed, realists have helped greatly to banish the now outworn notion that judges are only discovering the law when they are in fact engaged in judicial legislation. But few people will accept the proposition that a philosophy of law can be built upon the foundations the realists are able to lay.

Recent trends in jurisprudence show signs of a healthy development which has not yet attained full growth. If British jurists are still under the influence of Austin, their American colleagues are still dominated by Holmes. Social changes will continue to require creative legal thought to keep the law abreast of the environment

[21] See especially Llewellyn's book *The Bramble Bush* (New York, 1930). There are a great many articles by Llewellyn which can be found through use of the *Index to Legal Periodicals*.

[22] K. N. Llewellyn, *The Cheyenne Way* (Norman, Okla., 1941).

[23] *The Bramble Bush*, p. 3.

in which it operates. In a rapidly changing society the ideas of many men will contribute to the solution of problems, but these ideas must be organized if they are to be effective. Jurisprudence as the social science which deals primarily with the law is under special obligation to avail itself of all the help it can obtain from the other social sciences. Without co-operative effort among the social sciences, the aims and purposes of the law at any particular time cannot be formulated intelligently.

Index

Accursius, 6
Act of Settlement, 203
Aethelstan, 159
Agobard, Bishop, 97
Alaric, 89, 130
Alciat, 8, 129
Alfonso the Wise of Castile, 167
Alfred, King of England, 109, 110
Althusius, Johannes, 9, 45, 46, 65
Alwyn, Bishop of Winchester, 160
American Journal of Comparative Law, 215
Analytical school of jurisprudence, 12–20, 27, 207, 213–214
Appeal of Murder Act, 165
Aquinas, St. Thomas, 39–43, 46, 59–60, 67
Aristotle, 31, 42, 59, 72, 216
Ashford v. Thornton, 165
Assize utrum of 1164, 115
Assize of Clarendon, 115, 170, 171
Assizes of the Court of Burgesses of Jerusalem, 35
Augustine, St., 33–35, 36, 58
Aurelius, Marcus, 33
Austin, John, 12–18, 20, 27, 196, 207, 213, 214, 222
Avignon, 129
Azo, 194

Bacon, Sir Francis, 200
Bacon, Sir Nicholas, 199
Bagehot, Walter, 75
Barbaric Codes of Law, 88–89, 92–96
Bartolists, 8, 216
Bartolus of Sassoferrato, 7–8, 128, 129, 130, 183, 184
Baudouin, 9

Becket, St. Thomas á, 119
Bentham, Jeremy, 12, 52, 206, 207
Benthamism and the Benthamite Reforms, 206–207
Beyer, Georg, 136
Bill of Rights of 1689, 203
Blackstone, W., 14, 126, 175, 195, 199, 205, 206
Bloweberme, Walter, 164–165
Bodin, Jean, 48, 129
Bologna, Law School, 37, 107, 118, 119, 121, 127, 128
Bolognese glossators, 23, 27, 39, 95, 107, 128, 183, 184
Bourges, school, 8–9, 129
Bracton, Henry de, 23, 48, 108, 118, 121, 122–123, 124, 126, 173, 175, 193, 194, 197
Brandenberg, Elector of, 136
Brougham, 207
Buchanan, George, 44
Buckland, W. W., 141
Burke, Edmund, 21
Bushel's Case, 174–175

Canon law, 7, 57, 91, 93, 102–104, 106, 118, 119–121, 127, 133, 185
Canute, 150
Capitularies, 96–97
Caracalla, 81, 87, 186
Cassiodoris, 36
Celsus, 190
Charlemagne, 94, 95, 96, 97, 100, 103, 106, 113, 161, 167
Charles I, King of England, 201, 202
Charles II, King of England, 201–202, 203, 204
Cheyenne Indians, 222

INDEX

INDEX